VEGAN
Mac & Cheese

VEGAN
Mac & Cheese

More than **50** Delicious
Plant-Based Recipes for the
Ultimate Comfort Food

Robin Robertson

HARVARD
COMMON
PRESS

Inspiring | Educating | Creating | Entertaining

Brimming with creative inspiration, how-to projects, and useful information to enrich your everyday life, Quarto Knows is a favorite destination for those pursuing their interests and passions. Visit our site and dig deeper with our books into your area of interest: Quarto Creates, Quarto Cooks, Quarto Homes, Quarto Lives, Quarto Drives, Quarto Explores, Quarto Gifts, or Quarto Kids.

First Published in 2019 by The Harvard Common Press, an imprint of The Quarto Group, 100 Cummings Center, Suite 265-D, Beverly, MA 01915, USA.
T (978) 282-9590 F (978) 283-2742 QuartoKnows.com

The Harvard Common Press titles are also available at discount for retail, wholesale, promotional, and bulk purchase. For details, contact the Special Sales Manager by email at specialsales@quarto.com or by mail at The Quarto Group, Attn: Special Sales Manager, 100 Cummings Center, Suite 265-D, Beverly, MA 01915, USA.

23 22 21 20 19   1 2 3 4 5

ISBN: 978-1-55832-973-7

Digital edition published in 2019
eISBN: 978-1-55832-974-4

Library of Congress Cataloging-in-Publication Data available.

Photography: Jack Adams Photography
Food styling: Adriana Katekawa

Printed in China

FOR THE ANIMALS

Contents

Thinking Outside the Box

Vegan Mac & Cheese is a celebration of America's favorite comfort food, made healthy and delicious with innovative plant-based ingredients.

Macaroni and cheese has long been one of America's go-to comfort food meals. Warm, creamy, and delicious, it's one of the first grown-up foods enjoyed by young children. Whether our moms simply opened a box of dried noodles and a packet of orange powder, or made it from scratch with a béchamel sauce and four kinds of cheese, the end result was always flavorful, satisfying, and sustaining.

Most of us never outgrow that childhood fondness for mac and cheese, and happily pass the tradition of this inexpensive, homey meal to our kids and grandkids. Mac and cheese has a fancy side, too, often showing up on restaurant menus all dressed up with chunks of lobster meat or a dusting of white truffle.

As much as it is loved, classic macaroni and cheese has been off-limits to vegans and those who avoid dairy products due to allergies or other health issues—until now.

As many vegans can now attest, you don't need dairy cheese to make a sumptuous mac and cheese. In fact, you don't need cheese at all. Just ask the more than 3,000 people who attend the annual Vegan Mac 'n Cheese Smackdown in Baltimore, where as many as thirty chefs and caterers compete for the title of best vegan mac 'n' cheese. And that's what this book is about— the gentrifying, reclaiming, and veganizing of macaroni and cheese—or more accurately, a book of recipes for mac *un*cheese.

Whether you prefer your mac and cheese saucy or firm, stovetop or baked, you'll find lots to love in this book. The opening chapter provides my eight basic mac and cheese recipes, followed by chapters featuring vegetables such as Spinach-Artichoke Mac and Cheese (page 70), Arugula Pesto Mac Uncheese (page 78), and Buffalo Cauliflower Mac (page 75). The book also includes a chapter inspired by global flavors, such as Mac and Thai (page 46) and Creamy Curry Mac (page 59). There are enough recipes in this book to enjoy a different comforting mac and cheese every week of the year. When you factor in the numerous add-ins and topping ideas, this book opens the door to hundreds of possible recipe variations. What I found most fun in writing the book was sharing my special favorites.

A chapter titled "Meaty Macs" contains hearty casseroles such as Chili Mac (page 96), Brat & Kraut Mac & Cheese (page 110), and Philly Cheesesteak Mac (page 102) and features ingredients such as seitan, tofu, and tempeh. There are also many recipes that are completely soy free, gluten free, and nut free.

The final chapter includes some fun recipes using leftover mac and cheese, such as Mac Uncheese Balls (page 126), Mac Uncheese Quesadillas (page 133), and even Mac 'n' Pizza (page 131).

These mouthwatering recipes will appeal to vegans and omnivores alike, and they'll have kids of all ages saying, "Mac uncheese? Yes, please!"

THE MAC AND CHEESE STORY

Traditional macaroni and cheese has been hugely popular for decades, in no small part due to the commercial mixes and dairy-based cheeses and sauces that made them easy to make. Vegans don't eat dairy products so, for that reason, vegans abstained from that comforting mouthful of traditional mac and cheese. However, thanks to a handful of innovators over the past twenty years, truly satisfying dairy-free mac-and-cheese dishes have achieved an almost cult-like following among vegans. Vegan restaurants across the country now offer mac-and-cheese choices on their menus, and vegan mac-and-cheese festivals and contests pop up in cities across the country.

Before we dig into the recipes, let's take a look at how this comfort food favorite came to be, and the ingenious ways by which it is now being enjoyed in such excellent vegan versions. While some texts relate that macaroni and cheese had its beginnings in colonial America at a New England church supper, the dish actually has a much older history.

MACARONI AND CHEESE

Macaroni took a long journey before it partnered with cheese. Early Chinese texts reference noodle eating in 3000 BCE. In the first century, Etruscan noodles, called *lagane*, were made from the same durum wheat used today to make pasta, however, instead of boiling the noodles, they were baked. During the seventh through ninth centuries, pasta came to the Mediterranean region during the Arab conquests of Sicily. In 1271, Marco Polo brought pasta from China but, by then, pasta was already known in Italy. Which brings us to the question: How did macaroni and cheese become a thing? The chart on the next two pages provides a timeline.

A MACARONI AND CHEESE TIMELINE

1300s
The pasta and cheese dish traveled from Italy to France and then to England. A cheese and pasta casserole recipe was published in a French cookbook called *The Forme of Cury*, or *The Method of Cooking*.

1802
Jefferson hosted a state dinner that featured macaroni and cheese (then called macaroni pie) on the menu. Since then, the dish has been associated with the United States.

1200s
An Italian cookbook called *Liber de Coquina*, or *Book of Cooking*, includes a recipe called *de lasanis*, ostensibly the first macaroni and cheese recipe. The recipe calls for sheets of pasta cut into small squares, cooked in boiling water, and tossed with grated cheese.

1769
The Experienced English Housekeeper by Elizabeth Raffald featured the first modern recipe for a macaroni and cheese casserole.

1793
Thomas Jefferson enjoyed macaroni and cheese in France and Italy and then brought a recipe and pasta machine back to Virginia.

1824
A macaroni and cheese recipe appeared in the cookbook *The Virginia Housewife* by Mary Randolph.

Mid-1880s
Macaroni and cheese grew in popularity as it became both more affordable and accessible.

1937–Present
Macaroni and cheese remains popular today as the ultimate comfort food.

2019
Vegan Mac & Cheese by Robin Robertson was published. This is the first book devoted entirely to plant-based macaroni and cheese.

1852–1861
Recipes for macaroni and cheese were featured in *Hand-Book of the Useful Arts*, the *Godey's Lady's Book*, and *Mrs. Beeton's Book of Household Management*.

1937
Kraft Macaroni and Cheese Dinner first sold in grocery stores as "the housewife's best friend." More than 8 million boxes were sold in 1937 alone.

1994
The Uncheese Cookbook by vegan cheese pioneer Jo Stepaniak was published. The "cheesy-ness" of her mac and cheese was revolutionary and inspired many cooks, restaurants, and product developers to refine plant-based cheese.

VEGAN CHEESE: ORIGINS

If you Google "vegan mac and cheese," you will be inundated with countless recipes by food bloggers eager to share their version of the ultimate comfort food. And, while there's no official record of the first vegan mac and cheese, some credit surely goes to vegan dairy-alternative trailblazers such as Jo Stepaniak, author of the 1994 groundbreaking book, *The Uncheese Cookbook*, which contains her recipe for Macaroni and Cheez. Since that time, many general vegan cookbooks contain iterations of the dish.

Many years ago, commercial vegan cheese products became available, but sometimes the results were not very appealing. In the last several years, all that has changed with numerous plant-based cheese companies popping up all over, offering cheesy goodness to rival any dairy-based cheese. There are hard and soft cheeses. There are cheeses that spread, shred, slice, and melt. The following lists some of the most popular cheeses by company brand name.

Daiya: Often credited with the first truly meltable dairy-free shreds in a variety of flavors, this popular company also offers dairy-free cheese in slices, blocks, and spreads, as well as its own Cheezy Mac.

Field Roast: This company is the maker of the popular Vegan Chao Slices—a vegan coconut cheese alternative—perfect for grilled uncheese sandwiches.

Follow Your Heart: The company makes nondairy cheeses under the name Vegan Gourmet that include mozzarella, cheddar, nacho, Monterey Jack, garden herb, American, and provolone.

Kite Hill: Its artisanal nondairy cheese offerings include the creamy Soft Fresh Original, Soft Fresh Truffle Dill & Chive, and an aged soft ripened cheese with a delicate white rind. It also makes fresh ricotta and cultured cream cheese–style spreads.

Miyoko's Kitchen: This home of a variety of artisanal cheeses was developed by vegan cookbook author Miyoko Schinner. From delicate and creamy to pungent and hard, flavors include aged Sharp Farmhouse English, Black Ash, and Winter Truffle.

Tofutti: In addition to its popular Better Than Sour Cream and Better Than Cream Cheese, Tofutti also makes a plant-based ricotta and American and mozzarella slices.

Treeline Cheese: Its artisanal aged nut cheeses are firm, tangy, and creamy. Flavors include chipotle-serrano pepper, herb-garlic, and green peppercorn.

MAC AND CHEESE ON RESTAURANT MENUS

Vegan mac and cheese dishes are easy to find on the menus of vegan (and some nonvegan) restaurants throughout the world, such as the ones listed here (as of this writing).

Belmont Vegetarian, Worcester, Massachusetts
It serves an extra-saucy vegan mac and cheese made with a blend of plant milks and vegan cheddar.

by CHLOE, London, United Kingdom (also has U.S. locations)
Its popular vegan mac 'n' cheese is made with a sweet potato–cashew cheese sauce, shiitake bacon, and almond parmesan.

City Cakes & Café, Salt Lake City, Utah
Made with spiral noodles and roasted red peppers, cashews give the creamy sauce its rich flavor.

Cornbread Cafe, Eugene, Oregon
The creamy, cashew-based sauce for its mac and cheese is similar to a rich béchamel.

Detroit Vegan Soul, Detroit, Michigan
Its Soul Platter consists of vegan mac 'n' cheese, smoked collards, glazed yams, black-eyed peas, and corn bread.

Donna Jean, San Diego, California
This plant-based restaurant offers Cast Iron Mac & Trees, featuring smoked vegan cheddar, tomatoes, and chives.

Great Sage, Clarksville, Maryland
Its Adult Mac is a good reason to make a culinary pilgrimage to this small town in Maryland.

Grey Cells Green, Melbourne, Australia
Its vegan mac and cheese is macaroni smothered in a velvety cashew cheese sauce.

LOV, Montreal, Canada
This restaurant serves a kale mac'n'cheese made with casarecce pasta, squash, and sweet potato sauce with almond parmesan.

Modern Love, Brooklyn, New York
Its Mac & Shews is made with a creamy red pepper–cashew cheese and served with crusted tofu, blackened cauliflower, sautéed kale, and spiced pecans.

Plum Bistro, Seattle, Washington
In addition to a classic version, Plum Bistro also features a spicy Cajun mac and cheese—both are crispy on top and creamy inside.

The Loaded Bowl, Oklahoma City, Oklahoma
The menu features the Down Home Bowl, a variation on its popular Cashew Mac + Cheese, which is served with vegan barbecue.

Veganerie, Bangkok, Thailand
Its Vegan Mac & Cheese is made with chewy macaroni, a creamy cheesy sauce, nut parmesan, and crispy soy bacon.

MAKING MAC UNCHEESE AT HOME

There are a few key components to making a delicious mac uncheese. Foremost is the cheesy sauce—and the one component that separates a plant-based mac and cheese from a traditional dairy-based version. Once you decide on the type of sauce you want, pick a pasta shape (elbow macaroni is traditional). From there, decide on a topping (I like Toasted Panko Crumbs, page 25), and any add-ins you might like. Following is a discussion on each component.

THE UNCHEESE

It's the creamy cheesy sauce that makes macaroni and cheese such a popular dish, and there are a number of ways to achieve it without using dairy products.

NUTRITIONAL YEAST

If nutritional yeast is new to you, you may be wondering why this ingredient is included in so many recipes in this cookbook. The simple answer is that nutritional yeast provides a decidedly cheesy flavor, making it a natural choice and not-so-secret ingredient for making vegan cheese sauces taste cheesy.

Nutritional yeast is sold in most natural food stores and larger supermarkets. It is also available online. There are two types of nutritional yeast—unfortified and fortified. Always buy *fortified* nutritional yeast as it is an easy (and delicious) way to get vitamin B_{12} into a vegan diet.

Naturally low in sodium and calories, nutritional yeast is also fat free, sugar free, gluten free, and vegan. It is a complete protein, containing all nine essential amino acids that humans must get from food. Just 1 tablespoon (3.75 g) contains 2 grams of protein and is especially rich in thiamine, riboflavin, niacin, and vitamins B_6 and B_{12}. To preserve all the B vitamins, store nutritional yeast in a tightly sealed container to keep it protected from light and moisture.

IMPORTANT

All yeasts are not created equal. Check labels carefully—you want "nutritional yeast"—not "active dry yeast" or "brewer's yeast." (Active dry yeast is used to leaven bread and is still alive. Brewer's yeast is used to brew beer and tastes very bitter.)

QUICK CASHEW TIP

Instead of soaking cashews in advance, you can boil them for about 15 minutes and then drain well and they'll be softened enough to puree into a smooth sauce in a high-powered blender.

NOTE

If you don't have a high-powered blender, you can use a regular blender or food processor, but the results won't be as smooth.

SAUCY IDEAS

The cheesy sauces in these mac and cheese recipes can be enjoyed beyond their intended uses. You can skip the macaroni and toss the sauce with sliced potatoes for a dreamy scalloped potato dish, or pour it over baked potatoes, steamed veggies, or rice. The sauce also makes a great addition to nachos and can also be used as a dip for veggies, soft pretzels, and more.

VEGAN MAC & CHEESE SAUCES

Brat & Kraut Mac & Cheese sauce
see recipe page 110

Mom's Baked Mac Uncheese sauce
see recipe page 37

Cashew Cheesy Mac sauce
see recipe page 34

Brussels and Bacon Cheesy Mac sauce
see recipe page 85

In a pinch, use a shredded vegan cheese product to melt into your macaroni and, voilà, you have mac uncheese. However, I prefer to make my own cheesy sauce for a number of reasons:

1. **It's healthier.** Whole food plant-based sauces are better for you than processed vegan cheese products.

2. **It's cheaper.** Vegan cheese products can be costly—it's much less expensive to make your own.

3. **It tastes better.** The recipes for the various cheesy sauces in this book were specially developed to complement each particular recipe. They can also be adjusted according to your personal taste.

4. **You decide what goes in them.** If you are allergic to a particular ingredient, such as soy or cashews, it is possible to make a cheesy sauce without using these ingredients.

The cheesy sauces in this book are made using a variety of ingredients. The most common bases are made with the following blended with other ingredients, such as nutritional yeast, plant milk, vegetable broth, miso paste, lemon juice, and mustard.

1. **Roux:** Plant milk thickened with a roux made with vegan butter and flour. Always use a plain unsweetened plant milk—I typically use almond or soy milk.

2. **Cashew cream:** Soaked and drained cashews. Recipes are included for Cashew Cream (page 109), and Cheddary Sauce (page 103), which are called for in some recipes.

3. **Tofu:** Puréed tofu.

4. **Vegetables:** Puréed cooked vegetables such as potatoes, sweet potatoes, carrots, and winter squash.

NOTE

Most recipes in this book do not call for commercial vegan cheese products, but you can use them if you like. For example, make your cheese sauce even richer by stirring in some shredded vegan cheese, or blend some vegan butter or vegan cream cheese into virtually any recipe, if you're in the mood for extra decadence.

QUANTITY GUIDE

Here's a simple guide using elbow macaroni as an average or baseline (other types of pasta will measure more or less, depending on size and shape):

- 1 (16-ounce, or 454 g) box elbow macaroni = 4 cups dry pasta = 8 cups (1.1 kg) cooked pasta
- At least 4 cups (weight varies) of sauce is needed for 8 cups (1.1 kg) cooked pasta.
- A 9 × 13-inch (23 × 33 cm) or (preferably) a 10 × 14-inch (25 × 35 cm) baking dish is best for 8 cups (1.1 kg) cooked pasta + 4 to 6 cups (weight varies) sauce.

If your mac uncheese features add-ins, you will need a 10 × 14-inch (25 × 35 cm) or other 4-quart (3.8 L) baking dish. Otherwise, divide the mac uncheese into two 8- or 9-inch (20 or 23 cm) 2-quart (1.9 L) baking dishes.

If your cooked pasta yield is more than 8 cups (1.1 kg) or if you have a lot of add-ins or prefer a saucier dish, simply scoop out 1 or 2 cups (140 to 280 g) of the cooked pasta to make more room in the baking dish.

THE MAC

Although elbow macaroni is typically used (the ridged kind being preferable because it holds the sauce), there are a number of other pasta varieties that fill the bill nicely. Virtually any small pasta shape can be used interchangeably in any of the recipes. You can even use long noodles, if that is your preference.

Here are some of my favorite choices to put the "mac" in mac uncheese:

- Cavatappi/Cellentani
- Elbow macaroni
- Farfalle
- Orecchiette
- Penne
- Radiatore
- Campanelle
- Rotelle
- Rotini
- Small shells
- Ziti
- Gemelli

HOW MUCH PASTA?

Once upon a time, most boxes of pasta weighed 16 ounces (454 g). Then, seemingly overnight, some brands began selling their pasta varieties in 8-, 10-, and 12-ounce (225 g, 280 g, and 340 g) boxes, making the idea of calling for "a box of pasta" unrealistic. Still, it's also unrealistic to cook only a portion of a box of pasta. Why go through all the trouble of boiling and draining pasta more than once? Even if you don't plan to use it all in the same recipe, the leftover pasta can be used to make other dishes another day. I also dislike being fooled by half-empty boxes in my pantry, thinking they contain the full amount. To simplify things, I suggest you cook the entire box of pasta, regardless of weight, and then use as much or as little as needed for your recipe. Chances are, you'll end up using the whole box anyway.

Because most pasta still comes in 16-ounce (454 g) boxes, that is what is used in these recipes. If you prefer to make less, cut the recipe in half or make two smaller casseroles, saving one to serve later in the week.

TOPPINGS

A crunchy topping can be a textural and flavorful element that makes a mac uncheese extra special. It is an especially good idea to use a topping for baked mac uncheese casseroles because it keeps the pasta beneath it from drying out. Even when you're serving it from the stovetop (more on that later), a sprinkling of toasted crumbs or other topping makes a nice addition—both for visual appeal and added texture.

Here are a number of ways to top your mac:

Crumbs

- Cracker crumbs
- Crushed pretzels
- Herb-seasoned bread crumbs
- Toasted Panko Crumbs (page 25)
- Crushed cornflakes

Nuts/Seeds

- Chopped pecans, walnuts, or other chopped nuts
- Crushed smoked almonds

(continued on page 24)

Cavatappi/Cellentani

Orecchiette

Elbow macaroni

Penne

Farfalle

Radiatore

Campanelle

Small shells

Rotelle

Ziti

Rotini

Gemelli

- Roasted hulled pumpkin seeds
- Roasted hulled sunflower seeds
- Sesame seeds

Chips

- Crumbled barbecue potato chips
- Crumbled plain potato chips
- Crushed corn chips or tortilla chips

Seasonings

- Everything bagel seasoning
- Red pepper flakes
- Smoked paprika
- Tajín Clasico (chile-lime) seasoning
- Your favorite spice blend

Shredded Vegan Cheeses

- Cheddar
- Mozzarella
- Pepper Jack

Fresh Toppings

- Chopped fresh herbs
- Diced avocado
- Minced scallions

TOASTED PANKO

Panko, those wonderful Japanese bread crumbs, make an ideal crumb topping for mac uncheese. Trouble is, they're best when toasted until golden brown and that can be a problem when you're making a stovetop mac uncheese, or even if it's baked, chances are your mac uncheese will be dried out by the time those crumbs are brown enough.

The solution is simple: toast your panko in advance. You can then sprinkle them on your stovetop mac uncheese as well as the baked variation—a few more minutes in the oven will just make them better!

TOASTED PANKO CRUMBS

½ cup (25 g) panko bread crumbs

Here's a basic recipe for toasting panko crumbs.

1. Preheat the oven to 400°F (200°C).

2. Spread the panko on a rimmed baking sheet and bake for 3 to 4 minutes, or until the crumbs are lightly browned.

3. Remove and allow to cool. If not using right away, cool the toasted crumbs completely before transferring to a tightly sealed container. Store at room temperature.

Makes ½ cup (about 25 g)

ADD-INS

There are truly countless variations on the standard mac and cheese casserole by virtue of adding different ingredients. The most common ways to add a special nuance are to enrich the sauce or add another element to the dish, such as cooked vegetables or other ingredients. Here are some of my favorites:

Sauce Add-ins

- Balsamic syrup
- Chimichurri sauce
- Gochujang sauce
- Pesto
- Salsa
- Vegan Sour Cream (page 109)
- Sriracha, or other hot sauce
- Tamari
- Toasted sesame oil
- Truffle oil

Vegetable Add-ins

- Caramelized onions
- Chopped fresh tomatoes
- Chopped sun-dried tomatoes
- Chopped vegan bacon
- Cooked, chopped carrots, broccoli, or other vegetable
- Diced avocado
- Minced fresh chives, cilantro, parsley, or other herb
- Minced scallion

NATIONAL MAC AND CHEESE DAY

In the United States, July 14 is National Mac and Cheese Day—a day set aside to honor this classic comfort food.

- Pickled sliced jalapeños
- Pitted sliced Kalamata olives
- Roasted red peppers
- Sautéed mushrooms
- Shredded vegan cheese
- Thawed frozen green peas
- Vegan parmesan

STOVETOP VERSUS OVEN = SAUCY VERSUS FIRM

With mac and cheese, there are generally two camps when it comes to texture preference. Some people prefer it saucy while others prefer it firm. The recipes in this book are a combination of stovetop, baked, and stovetop with a baked variation.

As a rule, mac and cheese made on a stovetop and served right away will be saucier than those baked, simply because the pasta continues to absorb the sauce after it sits (or bakes) a while. The tradeoff is the saucier version should be made and served just before eating, while the baked variation can be assembled ahead of time, making it easier for company. Another factor is a crunchy topping, usually associated with baked versions.

To achieve the best of both worlds, make the sauce and macaroni for a stovetop version ahead of time, but wait to combine and heat it together closer to serving time. If you want a crunchy topping, simply make some Toasted Panko Crumbs (see page 25) and top the mac and cheese when ready to serve. If you prefer the baked method, but like it saucier, make 1 to 2 cups (weight varies) of extra sauce and pour some on the bottom of the casserole dish before adding the mac uncheese, and pour the remaining half on top before baking. Another option is to use a little less pasta than the recipe calls for—which will produce saucier results.

Some people like it when the top layer of mac uncheese is a little crusty, but to some crusty = dried out. You can prevent this if you toast your crumbs in advance and cover your baking dish with aluminum foil before baking.

PORTION SIZE

Most recipes in this book make 4 to 6 servings. This is based on the assumption that the mac and cheese is the main dish or perhaps served with a side salad or vegetable. The actual number of servings may differ based on the following factors:

- No two appetites are alike.
- The serving size depends on whether it's being served as a main dish or a side dish.
- The range allows for the inclusion of add-ins or other additional ingredients.

If you have leftovers, serve the remaining mac and cheese later in the week, either by simply reheating (you'll probably need to add some liquid) or transforming it into another dish using one of the recipes in chapter 5.

THE SECOND TIME AROUND

In my house we live for leftovers, so when I make a large pan of mac uncheese, visions of leftovers invariably dance in my head before the original dish is finished cooking. Not everyone loves eating the same thing twice in one week. Here are some solutions to repackage that original mac uncheese into a brand-new meal.

BAKING AND SINGLE-SERVE

To bake in a casserole: Transfer the mac and cheese into a greased 3- to 4-quart (2.8 to 3.8 L) baking dish, spreading it evenly. Sprinkle the top with crumbs. Bake at 350°F (180°C) for about 20 minutes until heated through and bubbling.

For individual gratin dishes: Spoon the mac and cheese into greased individual gratin dishes. Top with crumbs. Bake at 350°F (180°C) for about 20 minutes until heated through and bubbling.

Begin with a clean baking or serving dish. Transfer the leftover mac uncheese to the new dish and bring it to room temperature, or warm it for a minute or two in the microwave. Stir in a little soy or almond milk to give it a creamy texture and then work your magic by stirring in any of the following:

- 1 to 2 cups (weight varies)—creamy mushroom soup
- Chopped vegan bacon or vegan sausage
- Cooked veggies, such as roasted halved (or quartered) Brussels sprouts, chopped greens, chopped broccoli, and so on
- Curry paste, pesto, salsa, Thai chili paste, or gochujang sauce
- Canned or jarred diced green chiles

Other ideas include adding a new topping just before serving to make it look brand-new:

- Dust with ground toasted nuts
- Sprinkle on some crumbled potato chips or corn chips
- Top with diced avocado and a little hot sauce
- Sprinkle on your favorite spice blend

You can also use leftover mac and cheese to make the recipes in chapter 5 (pages 120–135). When you try one (or more) of these to jazz up your leftover mac, it may even be yummier the second time around.

"BROWNED AND BUBBLY ON TOP"

Here's a trick to give your stovetop mac uncheese that "browned and bubbly on top" look.

1. Transfer your cooked mac uncheese to a 9 × 13-inch (23 × 33 cm) baking dish.

2. Top with a mixture of shredded vegan cheese and bread crumbs or cracker crumbs (about ½ cup [60 g]).

3. Spray top with cooking oil.

4. Place the baking dish about 4 inches (10 cm) under a preheated broiler.

5. Broil until browned and bubbly, 1 to 2 minutes. Serve.

CHAPTER 1

Basic Vegan Mac and Cheese

There is more than one way to achieve the creamy saucy goodness that goes into mac uncheese. Whether you prefer a classic roux-based sauce, one made with cashew cream, or a sauce made with blended cooked vegetables, these basic cheesy macs are the ones to choose when you want a no-frills mac uncheese, or one you can use to build your own favorite.

SOY-GOOD MAC UNCHEESE

Pasta

Vegan butter or cooking oil spray, for preparing the baking dish

16 ounces (454 g) elbow macaroni, or other small pasta

Sauce

1 (12-ounce, or 349 g) package silken tofu

1 cup (240 ml) plain unsweetened nondairy milk

¾ cup (45 g) nutritional yeast

2 tablespoons (28 g) vegan butter

2 tablespoons (30 ml) tamari

2 teaspoons prepared yellow mustard

1½ teaspoons paprika, divided

1 teaspoon onion powder

1 teaspoon garlic powder

¾ to 1 teaspoon salt

Topping

½ cup (25 g) Toasted Panko Crumbs (page 25), or your favorite topping

The sauce in this basic baked mac and cheese gets it creaminess from protein-rich tofu. Nutritional yeast lends a cheesy flavor.

1. **To make the pasta:** Preheat the oven to 350°F (180°C). Coat a 9 × 13-inch (23 × 33 cm) baking dish with vegan butter or spray it with cooking oil. Set aside.

2. Bring a large pot of salted water to a boil over high heat. Add the pasta and cook according to the package directions until al dente. Reserve 1 cup (240 ml) of the pasta cooking water. Drain the pasta and transfer it to the prepared baking dish.

3. **To make the sauce:** In a blender or food processor, combine the tofu, reserved cooking water, milk, nutritional yeast, butter, tamari, mustard, 1 teaspoon of paprika, the onion powder, garlic powder, and salt. Blend until completely smooth. Pour the cheese sauce over the pasta, gently stirring to combine.

4. **To finish:** Sprinkle the top with the toasted panko and the remaining ½ teaspoon of paprika. Cover the baking dish with aluminum foil and bake for 20 minutes. Serve hot.

Makes 4 to 6 servings

FREE MAC

Sauce

3 cups (720 ml) vegetable broth, plus more as needed

½ cup (80 g) chopped yellow onion

1 large carrot, chopped

1 large russet potato, peeled and cut into ½-inch (1 cm) dice

1 garlic clove, chopped

½ teaspoon ground turmeric

½ teaspoon paprika

Salt, to taste

Ground black pepper, to taste

½ cup (130 g) cooked or canned cannellini beans, or other white beans, drained

½ cup (120 ml) plain unsweetened nondairy milk, plus more as needed

⅓ cup (20 g) nutritional yeast

2 tablespoons (30 ml) fresh lemon juice

2 teaspoons Dijon mustard

Pasta

16 ounces (454 g) gluten-free elbow macaroni, or other small pasta

Topping

½ cup (60 g) gluten-free bread crumbs, toasted, or your favorite topping (optional)

Sriracha, for topping (optional)

This creamy casserole is free of soy, gluten, nuts, oil, and, of course, cheese. To make it a one-dish meal, stir in 2 cups (weight varies) of a steamed green vegetable, such as broccoli florets or chopped spinach. For a silky-smooth sauce, it is best to use a high-speed blender such as a Vitamix or Blend Tec.

1. **To make the sauce:** In a large saucepan over medium heat, warm the vegetable broth. Add the onion, carrot, potato, garlic, turmeric, and paprika. Season with salt and pepper. Bring to a boil, cover the pan, and cook until the vegetables are soft, 10 to 15 minutes. Remove from the heat and transfer to a high-speed blender.

2. To the cooked vegetables, add the beans, milk, nutritional yeast, lemon juice, and mustard. Blend until smooth. Taste and adjust the seasoning, as needed. If the sauce is too thick, add up to ½ cup (120 ml) more broth or milk. Set aside.

3. **To make the pasta:** Bring a large pot of salted water to a boil over high heat. Add the pasta and cook according to the package directions until al dente. Drain well and return it to the pot.

4. Add the sauce to the macaroni and gently stir to combine well.

5. **To finish:** Serve hot sprinkled with toasted crumbs and drizzled with sriracha (if using).

Makes 4 to 6 servings

BAKED VARIATION

Preheat the oven to 350°F (180°C) and coat a 9 × 13-inch (23 × 33 cm) baking dish with vegan butter or spray it with cooking oil. Transfer the mac uncheese to the prepared baking dish. Sprinkle with the toasted crumbs (if using), and bake until hot and golden on top, about 20 minutes. Serve immediately, drizzled with sriracha (if using).

CASHEW CHEESY MAC

Pasta
16 ounces (454 g) elbow macaroni

Sauce
¾ cup (135 g) chopped roasted
    red bell pepper
¾ cup (105 g) unsalted raw cashews,
    soaked in hot water for 30 minutes
    and drained
1½ cups (360 ml) plain unsweetened
    nondairy milk, divided
⅓ cup (20 g) nutritional yeast, plus
    more as needed
2 tablespoons (30 ml) fresh
    lemon juice
2 teaspoons white miso paste
1 teaspoon prepared yellow mustard
½ teaspoon onion powder
½ teaspoon smoked paprika
½ teaspoon salt, plus more as needed
¼ teaspoon ground black pepper

Topping
Toasted Panko Crumbs
    (page 25, optional)

The richly flavored sauce in this cheesy mac begins with blended soaked cashews. It gets some color (and extra flavor) from roasted red bell pepper and cheesy goodness from nutritional yeast.

1. **To make the pasta:** Bring a large pot of salted water to a boil over high heat. Add the pasta and cook according to the package directions until al dente. Drain well and return it to the pot.

2. **To make the sauce:** In a high-speed blender, combine the bell pepper, cashews, and 1 cup (240 ml) of milk. Blend until smooth.

3. Add the remaining ½ cup (120 ml) of milk, the nutritional yeast, lemon juice, miso, mustard, onion powder, paprika, salt, and pepper. Process until smooth and well blended. Taste and add more salt, as needed. Pour the sauce over the cooked pasta, place the pot over low heat, and gently stir to combine and heat through.

4. **To finish:** Serve hot, sprinkled with Toasted Panko Crumbs (if using).

Makes 4 to 6 servings

BAKED VARIATION

Preheat the oven to 350°F (180°C). Transfer the macaroni mixture to a greased 3½- to 4-quart (3.3 to 3.8 L) baking dish, sprinkle with Toasted Panko Crumbs (if using), cover the baking dish with aluminum foil, and bake for 15 minutes until heated through.

MOM'S BAKED MAC UNCHEESE

Pasta

16 ounces (454 g) elbow macaroni

Olive oil or vegan butter, for preparing the baking dish

Sauce

4 tablespoons (56 g) vegan butter

¼ cup (31 g) all-purpose flour

5 cups (1.2 L) plain unsweetened nondairy milk

1 teaspoon salt

⅓ cup (20 g) nutritional yeast, plus more as needed

1 teaspoon dry mustard

1 teaspoon onion powder

¼ teaspoon ground black pepper

1 cup (112 g) shredded vegan cheese (optional)

Topping

1 cup (72 g) finely crushed Ritz crackers

½ teaspoon paprika

1 tablespoon (15 ml) melted vegan butter

My mother used to make a delicious baked macaroni and cheese topped with (accidentally vegan) Ritz cracker crumbs and paprika. The sauce began with a roux to make a rich béchamel and was baked to perfection. Note: The texture of this baked casserole is meant to be firm, not saucy. The optional shredded vegan cheese makes the sauce richer, but it's delicious without it.

1. **To make the pasta:** Bring a large pot of salted water to a boil over high heat. Add the pasta and cook according to the package directions until al dente. Reserve 1 cup (240 ml) of pasta cooking water. Drain the pasta and set aside.

2. Preheat the oven to 350°F (180°C). Lightly grease a 9 × 13-inch (23 × 33 cm) baking dish with olive oil or vegan butter. Set aside.

3. **To make the sauce:** In a large saucepan over medium heat, melt the butter.

4. Whisk in the flour and cook, whisking, for 2 minutes. Whisk in the milk. Add the salt. Simmer, whisking occasionally, until thick, about 5 minutes.

5. Add the nutritional yeast, mustard, onion powder, and pepper and whisk until smooth. Cook for 5 minutes until thick. Reduce the heat to low. Taste and adjust the seasoning, as needed. If the sauce is too thick, add as much of the 1 cup (240 ml) of reserved cooking water, as desired.

6. Add the cooked macaroni to the sauce and stir to combine.

7. In a small bowl, stir together the cracker crumbs, paprika, and melted butter to combine.

8. **To finish:** Transfer the pasta mixture to the prepared baking dish, top with the cracker crumb mixture, and bake for 20 minutes, or until bubbly and golden on top.

Makes 4 to 6 servings

CLASSY MAC UNCHEESE

Pasta
16 ounces (454 g) gemelli, or other small pasta

Sauce
3 tablespoons (45 ml) olive oil, or (42 g) vegan butter

¼ cup (31 g) all-purpose flour

3½ cups (840 ml) plain unsweetened nondairy milk

¼ cup (15 g) nutritional yeast, plus more as needed

3 tablespoons (45 ml) dry white wine

2 tablespoons (32 g) almond butter

1 tablespoon (15 ml) fresh lemon juice

1 teaspoon Dijon mustard

½ teaspoon onion powder

½ teaspoon ground turmeric

½ teaspoon salt, plus more as needed

Topping
½ cup (48 g) coarsely ground almonds or walnuts, toasted

Truffle oil, for serving

Imbued with truffle oil, white wine, and almond butter, one taste will tell you this isn't an everyday mac uncheese. It's elegant enough to serve as a side dish for a special meal or, with the addition of sautéed mushrooms, cooked chard, or other add-ins, a delicious main dish.

1. **To make the pasta:** Bring a large pot of salted water to a boil over high heat. Add the pasta and cook according to the package directions until al dente. Drain well and return it to the pot.

2. **To make the sauce:** In a medium saucepan over medium heat, heat the olive oil.

3. Stir in the flour. Cook, stirring, until the flour begins to bubble. Slowly whisk in the milk. Cook, whisking, until the mixture is smooth and comes just to a simmer, about 5 minutes.

4. Reduce the heat to low and stir in the nutritional yeast, wine, almond butter, lemon juice, mustard, onion powder, turmeric, and salt, stirring until well blended. Taste and add more salt, as needed. Add the sauce to the cooked pasta and toss to combine and coat the pasta.

5. **To finish:** Serve hot, topped with toasted almonds and a drizzle of truffle oil.

Makes 4 to 6 servings

BAKED VARIATION

Preheat the oven to 350°F (180°C). Spray a large baking dish with nonstick cooking oil spray. Transfer the mac uncheese mixture to the prepared baking dish. Top with the almonds, cover the baking dish with aluminum foil, and bake for 15 to 20 minutes. Serve hot, drizzled with a little truffle oil.

ONE-POT CHEESY MAC

Pasta

16 ounces (454 g) elbow macaroni, or
    other small pasta

Sauce

2 cups (480 ml) water

1 large russet potato, peeled and diced

1 small carrot, chopped

½ of a small yellow onion, chopped

1 large garlic clove, smashed

¾ cup (105 g) unsalted raw cashews

Salt, to taste

½ cup (30 g) nutritional yeast

2 tablespoons (28 g) vegan butter
    (optional)

1 tablespoon (15 ml) fresh lemon juice

1 teaspoon cider vinegar

½ teaspoon prepared yellow mustard

¼ teaspoon ground turmeric

¼ teaspoon smoked paprika

Ground black pepper, to taste

Toasted Panko Crumbs (page 25), or
    your favorite topping (optional)

I love to cook but hate to wash dishes so, whenever I can, I reuse the same pot, as I do in this recipe. Simply cook the pasta, drain, and set aside while you make the sauce in the same pot. You then add the cooked pasta to the sauce, stir to coat and heat through, and dinner is served.

1. **To make the pasta:** Bring a large pot of salted water to a boil over high heat. Add the pasta and cook according to the package directions until al dente. Drain well and set aside.

2. **To make the sauce:** In the same pot, combine the water, potato, carrot, onion, garlic, cashews, and salt. Bring to a boil over high heat, then reduce the heat to maintain a simmer. Cover the pot and cook until the vegetables are soft, 10 to 15 minutes.

3. Carefully transfer the mixture to a high-speed blender. Add the nutritional yeast, butter (if using), lemon juice, vinegar, mustard, turmeric, and paprika. Season with salt and pepper. Blend until completely smooth, stopping to scrape down the sides, as needed.

4. Return the pasta to the pot. Pour the sauce over the pasta and gently stir to combine and coat the pasta with the sauce. Taste and adjust the seasoning, as needed. Place the pot over low heat and cook until hot.

5. **To finish:** Serve hot, sprinkled with Toasted Panko Crumbs (if using).

Makes 4 to 6 servings

GIVE THE GIFT OF MAC UNCHEESE

Assemble a "do-it-yourself" mac uncheese kit for a unique gift idea. Combine the dry mix ingredients from the Better-than-Boxed Mac Uncheese (page 42) and put the mix in a pretty lidded jar or resealable plastic bag. Gather the container of dry mix , a box of elbow macaroni (or your favorite pasta), a quart (960 ml) of shelf-stable unsweetened soy or almond milk, and some Tajín seasoning or smoked paprika. Arrange the components in a decorative basket, box, or, if you want to make it really special, put everything inside a large baking dish. Tuck in a copy of the recipe (or, better yet, a copy of this cookbook).

EASY-CHEESY PANTRY MAC

Pasta

16 ounces (454 g) penne, or other
    small pasta

Sauce

1¾ cups (273 g) rolled oats

½ cup (30 g) nutritional yeast

2 tablespoons (15 g) tapioca starch, or
    (16 g) cornstarch

1¾ teaspoons salt

1½ teaspoons onion powder

½ teaspoon smoked paprika

¼ teaspoon ground turmeric

1 (12-ounce, or 340 g) jar roasted red
    bell peppers, drained

1½ tablespoons (23 ml) fresh lemon
    juice

½ teaspoon yellow mustard

3¾ cups (900 ml) hot water

Your favorite add-ins (see page 26;
    optional)

Your favorite toppings (see page 21;
    optional)

Put your pasta in the boiling water and the easy-cheesy sauce will be ready by the time your pasta is done. Best of all, the sauce is made with on-hand pantry ingredients and is nut free and soy free. If you need the dish to be gluten free, use gluten-free pasta.

1. **To make the pasta:** Bring a large pot of salted water to a boil over high heat. Add the pasta and cook according to the package directions until al dente. Drain well and return it to the pot.

2. **To make the sauce:** In a blender or food processor, combine the oats, nutritional yeast, tapioca starch, salt, onion powder, paprika, and turmeric. Blend until the oats are a fine powder.

3. Add the bell peppers, lemon juice, mustard, and hot water. Blend until the sauce is smooth and begins to thicken, about 3 minutes. Taste and adjust the seasoning, as needed. Add the sauce to the cooked pasta and toss to coat. Place the pot over low heat and cook, stirring continually, for 2 to 3 minutes, or until hot.

4. Stir in your favorite add-ins (if using).

5. Serve hot sprinkled with your favorite topping (if using).

Makes 4 to 6 servings

BETTER-THAN-BOXED MAC UNCHEESE

Dry Mix

¾ cup (45 g) nutritional yeast
⅓ cup (40 g) tapioca starch
1½ teaspoons paprika
1½ teaspoons salt
1½ teaspoons onion powder
1 teaspoon garlic powder
½ teaspoon ground turmeric
½ teaspoon smoked paprika
½ teaspoon ground black pepper
¼ teaspoon dry mustard powder

Mac Uncheese

16 ounces (454 g) elbow macaroni
4 cups (960 ml) plain unsweetened
    nondairy milk
Tajín Clasico Seasoning (or other chili-
    lime seasoning blend), or smoked
    paprika, for topping

The dry mix can be made in advance for a quick and convenient mac uncheese anytime you like. Keep the mix on hand, along with a box of pasta and a quart (960 ml) of shelf-stable nondairy milk in an aseptic container and you'll always have a satisfying meal at your fingertips. I especially like topping this mac uncheese with Tajín Clasico Seasoning (available in most supermarkets) for its zesty—but not hot—chile-lime flavor.

1. **To make the dry mix:** In a medium lidded jar or other container with a tight-fitting lid, combine all the dry mix ingredients. Stir or cover and shake well to combine. Set aside or store at room temperature until needed.

2. **To make the mac uncheese:** Bring a large pot of salted water to a boil over high heat. Add the pasta and cook according to the package directions until al dente. Drain well and set aside.

3. Return the pot to medium-high heat and add 3 cups (720 ml) of the milk and dry mix, whisking to combine. Cook, whisking constantly, to thicken, about 3 minutes.

4. Add the reserved macaroni to the sauce and stir to combine and heat through. If the mixture is too thick, add the remaining 1 cup (240 ml) milk, a little at a time.

5. Serve hot, sprinkled with Tajín seasoning.

Makes 4 to 6 servings

CHAPTER 2

Global Cheesy Macs

The United States isn't the only country that knows its way around a pasta casserole. Germany has its käsespätzle; Barbados has a Bajan macaroni pie; Greece has pastitsio; and, of course, Italy has baked ziti. In addition to my own vegan spins on international classics, I've taken the liberty of creating some new combinations that will dazzle the palate—from Creamy Curry Mac (page 59) to zesty Salsa Mac and Queso (page 57).

MAC AND THAI

Sauce
2 teaspoons neutral vegetable oil
1 small yellow onion, minced
3 tablespoons (30 g) Thai red
    curry paste
½ teaspoon salt
¼ teaspoon ground black pepper
2 cups (480 ml) water, divided
¾ cup (105 g) unsalted raw cashews,
    soaked in boiling water for
    30 minutes, drained
1 (13-ounce, or 368 g) can unsweetened
    coconut milk

Pasta
16 ounces (454 g) gemelli, or other
    small pasta

Garnish
Chopped roasted peanuts
Fresh Thai basil, or chopped
    fresh cilantro
Red pepper flakes (optional)

Lime wedges, for serving

There's a lot to love about this culinary fusion-fest featuring gemelli pasta cloaked in a creamy sauce made with cashews, coconut milk, and Thai red curry paste.

1. **To make the sauce:** In a skillet over medium heat, heat the vegetable oil.

2. Add the onion and cook until tender, about 5 minutes.

3. Stir in the curry paste, salt, and pepper. Cook, stirring constantly, for 1 minute.

4. Stir in 1 cup (240 ml) of water and remove the skillet from the heat.

5. In a high-speed blender, combine the cashews and remaining 1 cup (240 ml) of water. Blend until completely smooth. Add the curry mixture and blend again until smooth. Set aside.

6. **To make the pasta:** Bring a large pot of salted water to a boil over high heat. Add the pasta and cook according to the package directions until al dente. Drain well and return it to pot.

7. **To finish:** Stir in the curry sauce and coconut milk. Place the pot over low heat and cook, stirring occasionally, for a few minutes to heat through and thicken the sauce. Taste and adjust the seasoning, as needed. Transfer to a large serving dish and serve hot, sprinkled with peanuts, basil, and red pepper flakes (if using), with lime wedges on the side for squeezing.

Makes 4 to 6 servings

VARIATION

For an even heartier (and more colorful) dish, add some cooked veggies, such as stir-fried chopped red bell pepper, carrot, broccoli, or snow peas.

KÄSESPÄTZLE

4 to 5 cups (616 to 770 g) cooked
Vegan Spätzle (page 50) or
store-bought
2 tablespoons (30 ml) olive oil, plus
more for preparing the baking dish
1 large yellow onion, chopped
Salt, to taste
Ground black pepper, to taste
4 tablespoons (56 g) vegan butter
¼ cup (31 g) all-purpose flour
1 cup (240 ml) vegetable broth
3 cups (720 ml) plain unsweetened
nondairy milk
½ to 1 teaspoon salt
¼ cup (15 g) nutritional yeast
1 teaspoon dry mustard
¾ teaspoon onion powder
¼ teaspoon ground black pepper
Minced fresh chives, chopped fresh
parsley or dill, or caramelized
onions, for garnish

This German version of macaroni and cheese is made with spätzle baked with cheese and caramelized onions and is a favorite comfort food in Germany. If using homemade spätzle (see page 50), you can make it ahead of time and refrigerate it until ready to use. Similarly, make the entire casserole ahead and reheat when needed. (Bring it to room temperature before baking.)

1. Prepare the spätzle and set aside. Coat a 3- to 4-quart (2.8 to 3.8 L) baking dish with olive oil. Set aside.

2. In a large skillet over medium-low heat, heat the olive oil.

3. Add the onion and cook, stirring occasionally, until soft and lightly browned, about 10 minutes. Season with salt and pepper. Set aside.

4. Preheat the oven to 350°F (180°C).

5. In a large saucepan over medium heat, melt the butter.

6. Whisk in the flour and cook, whisking, for 2 minutes. Whisk in the broth and milk. Add ½ to 1 teaspoon of salt (depending on the saltiness of your broth) and simmer, whisking occasionally, for about 5 minutes.

7. Add the nutritional yeast, mustard, onion powder, and pepper, whisking until smooth. Cook for 5 minutes until thick. Reduce the heat to low. Taste and adjust the seasoning, as needed.

8. Layer one-third of the cooked onions in the bottom of the prepared baking dish. Spread one-third of the cooked spätzle on top of the onions and sprinkle with one-third of the sauce, seasoning each layer with salt and pepper as you go. Repeat the layering with another one-third of the ingredients. For the final layer, begin with the spätzle, followed by the onions, and ending with the sauce. Bake for 15 minutes or until slightly browned on top.

Makes 4 to 6 servings

NOTE

If you'd like to garnish this dish with caramelized onion, cook an extra ½ cup (80 g) or so of chopped onion until caramelized and reserve it before proceeding with the recipe.

VEGAN SPÄTZLE

1¾ cups (217 g) all-purpose unbleached flour
¼ cup (30 g) chickpea flour
½ teaspoon salt
1½ cups (360 ml) plain unsweetened nondairy milk

You don't need a special contraption to make spätzle (although use it if you've got it!). All you need is a potato ricer or a colander with large holes to push the dumpling mixture through and into the water.

1. In a medium bowl, stir together the all-purpose flour, chickpea flour, and salt, mixing well.

2. Add the milk, whisking until you have a smooth, thick batter. Set aside for 20 minutes.

3. Bring a large pot of salted water to a boil over high heat. Place a colander or other perforated utensil over the boiling water and put about 1 cup (about 170 g) of the spätzle batter into the colander. Using the back of a large spoon, press the batter through the holes into the water. When the little dumplings float to the top, use a large slotted spoon to remove them from the water and set aside. Repeat with the remaining batter.

Makes about 4 cups (616 g)

GREEK SPINACH ORZO BAKE

Pasta

Nonstick cooking oil spray, for preparing the baking dish

16 ounces (454 g) orzo pasta

4 cups (120 g) packed fresh baby spinach

½ cup (75 g) crumbled tofu feta (recipe on page 53), drained

2 tablespoons (20 g) minced scallion

1 teaspoon finely grated lemon zest

Sauce

¼ cup (60 ml) olive oil

¼ cup (31 g) all-purpose flour

3 cups (720 ml) plain unsweetened nondairy milk

½ cup (120 ml) vegetable broth, plus more as needed

1 teaspoon salt

1 teaspoon dried oregano

1 teaspoon dry mustard

¼ teaspoon ground black pepper, plus more for seasoning

½ cup (75 g) crumbled tofu feta (recipe on page 53), drained

1 tablespoon (15 ml) fresh lemon juice, plus more for serving

This flavorful dish pays homage to popular Greek ingredients including lemon, orzo, spinach, (vegan) feta, and oregano.

1. Preheat the oven to 350°F (180°C). Lightly coat a 9 × 13-inch (23 × 33 cm) baking dish with cooking oil spray. Set aside.

2. **To make the pasta:** Bring a large pot of salted water to a boil over high heat. Add the pasta and cook according to the package directions until al dente. Drain well and transfer to a large bowl.

3. Stir in the spinach, feta, scallion, and lemon zest and set aside.

4. **To make the sauce:** In a large saucepan over medium heat, heat the olive oil.

5. Add the flour and cook, whisking, for 1 minute.

6. Whisk in the milk, broth, salt, and oregano. Simmer, whisking occasionally, until thick, about 5 minutes. Add the mustard and pepper and whisk until smooth. Cook for 5 minutes until very thick.

7. Reduce the heat to low. Stir in the feta and lemon juice. Taste and adjust the seasoning, as needed. If the sauce is too thick, add up to 1 cup (240 ml) more broth, as desired. Toss the sauce with the reserved orzo mixture and transfer to the prepared baking dish. Cover the baking dish with aluminum foil and bake for 20 minutes.

8. Serve hot with an extra squeeze of lemon juice and a few grinds of black pepper.

Makes 4 to 6 servings

TOFU FETA

8 ounces (225 g) extra-firm tofu,
    drained, patted dry, and cut into
    ½-inch (1 cm) cubes
⅓ cup (80 ml) olive oil
⅓ cup (80 ml) fresh lemon juice
2 garlic cloves, crushed
1 teaspoon salt
½ teaspoon dried oregano

Extra-firm tofu takes on the flavor of feta when soaked in a lemony garlic marinade. Use it in the Greek Spinach Orzo Bake on page 51 or add it to a Greek salad. For a more intense flavor, allow the tofu to marinate overnight.

Place the tofu cubes in a shallow bowl. Add the olive oil, lemon juice, garlic, salt, and oregano and toss to combine. Set aside to marinate for 30 minutes, turning once halfway through. The tofu feta is now ready to remove from the marinade and use.

Makes about 1½ cups (8 ounces, or 225 g) tofu feta cubes

BLUSHING BAKED ZITI

1 tablespoon (15 ml) olive oil

1 yellow onion, chopped

2 garlic cloves, minced

¼ cup (60 ml) water

2 tablespoons (7.5 g) nutritional yeast

1 tablespoon (17 g) white miso paste

¾ teaspoon salt

Ground black pepper, to taste

3 tablespoons (45 ml) fresh
    lemon juice

12 ounces (340 g) extra-firm tofu,
    drained

16 ounces (454 g) ziti, or other
    small pasta

4 cups (1 kg) marinara sauce

2 tablespoons (16 g) Nut Parm
    (page 55)

Red pepper flakes (optional)

Handful fresh basil leaves,
    chopped (optional)

Baked ziti, made with tomato sauce and dollops of ricotta cheese, is an Italian classic. I change it up a bit here, layering a creamy white sauce over the marinara. The resulting sauce is light red in color, hence the "blush."

1. In a skillet over medium heat, heat the olive oil.

2. Add the onion and cook for 4 to 5 minutes, or until softened. Stir in the garlic and cook for 1 minute more. Stir in the water, nutritional yeast, miso, and salt and season with pepper. Set aside.

3. Crumble the tofu into a food processor. Add the onion-garlic mixture and lemon juice and blend until smooth, stopping to scrape down the sides, as needed.

4. Bring a large pot of salted water to a boil over high heat. Add the pasta and cook according to the package directions until al dente. Drain well and set aside.

5. Preheat the oven to 375°F (190°C).

6. Spread a thin layer of marinara sauce into the bottom of a 9 × 13-inch (23 × 33 cm) baking dish. Spread half the cooked pasta on top, then pour half the remaining marinara sauce over the pasta. Spoon half the tofu mixture onto the pasta. Repeat with the remaining pasta and marinara sauce. Spread the remaining tofu mixture over the pasta and sauce. Sprinkle the Nut Parm on top. Tightly cover the baking dish with aluminum foil and bake for 20 minutes.

7. Remove the foil and bake for 10 minutes more, or until hot and lightly browned.

8. Serve garnished with a few shakes of red pepper flakes and the basil (if using).

Makes 4 to 6 servings

NUT PARM

1 cup (145 g) unsalted blanched
    almonds, or (140 g) unsalted
    raw cashews
⅓ cup (20 g) nutritional yeast
½ teaspoon salt
¼ teaspoon onion powder

Keep a supply of this condiment on hand to shake on your favorite mac uncheese (or other pasta dishes) with abandon.

Combine all the ingredients in a food processor and pulse until the mixture has a fine crumbly texture, stopping to scrape down the sides, as needed. Transfer to a shaker jar or other container with a tight lid. Store in the refrigerator.

Makes about 1⅓ cups (about 170 g)

ITALIAN MACARONI PIE

Pasta

16 ounces (454 g) dried spaghetti

Sauce

Nonstick cooking spray, for preparing
   the baking dish

2 tablespoons (30 ml) olive oil

1 small yellow onion, chopped

2 garlic cloves, minced

12 ounces (340 g) silken tofu, drained

⅓ cup (20 g) nutritional yeast

2 tablespoons (28 g) vegan butter

2 tablespoons (30 ml) fresh
   lemon juice

1 tablespoon (17 g) white miso paste

1 teaspoon onion powder

1 teaspoon garlic powder

1 teaspoon salt, plus more as needed

½ to ¾ teaspoon ground black pepper,
   plus more as needed

2½ cups (600 ml) plain unsweetened
   nondairy milk

½ cup (30 g) chopped fresh parsley
   (optional)

The traditional version of this dish is called *cacio e pepe*, or "cheese and pepper," for the copious amounts of Pecorino-Romano cheese and black pepper used in the dish. It is usually made in a large round pan and sliced into wedges. You can use a 9- or 10-inch (23 or 25 cm) springform pan—just tightly wrap the bottom with aluminum foil to prevent leaks.

1. **To make the pasta:** Bring a large pot of salted water to a boil over high heat. Add the pasta and cook according to the package directions until al dente. Drain well and return it to the pot.

2. **To make the sauce:** Preheat the oven to 375°F (190°C). Lightly coat a 9- or 10-inch (23 or 25 cm) springform pan or large baking dish with cooking spray. If using a springform pan, tightly wrap the bottom with aluminum foil and set the pan on a rimmed baking sheet. Set aside.

3. In a small skillet over medium heat, heat the olive oil. Add the onion and garlic and cook, stirring, until soft, about 5 minutes. Remove from the heat and set aside.

4. In a blender or food processor, combine the tofu, nutritional yeast, butter, lemon juice, miso, onion powder, garlic powder, salt, and pepper. Add the onion mixture and milk and blend until completely smooth and creamy. Taste and add more salt, as needed. Add the sauce to the cooked pasta, stirring to coat. Transfer the mixture to the prepared baking dish, smoothing the top. Bake for about 20 minutes until golden.

5. Turn on the broiler and brown the top of the pie, watching carefully to prevent burning. Remove from the oven and set aside for about 10 minutes before removing the sides of the springform pan.

6. Sprinkle the top with parsley (if using) and season with pepper, if desired. Cut into wedges and serve warm.

Makes 4 to 6 servings

SALSA MAC AND QUESO

Pasta
16 ounces (454 g) elbow macaroni, or other small pasta

Sauce
1 large russet potato, diced
1 small yellow onion, diced
1 small red bell pepper, diced
1 jalapeño pepper, seeded and chopped
1 garlic clove, chopped
½ cup (70 g) unsalted raw cashews
1½ cups (360 ml) vegetable broth
Salt, to taste
¾ cup (180 ml) plain unsweetened nondairy milk
3 tablespoons (11 g) nutritional yeast, plus more as needed
1 tablespoon (17 g) white miso paste
½ teaspoon ground cumin
¼ teaspoon ground turmeric
¾ cup (195 g) tomato salsa (mild, medium, or spicy)
1 tablespoon (15 ml) fresh lemon juice

Toppings
1 cup (63 g) crushed tortilla chips, or corn chips
1 ripe tomato, diced
1 ripe Hass avocado, peeled, pitted, and diced

A creamy dairy-free queso sauce and your favorite tomato salsa team up deliciously in this zesty mac casserole. Top with diced tomato, avocado, and tortilla chips for the ultimate flavor experience.

1. **To make the pasta:** Bring a large pot of salted water to a boil over high heat. Add the pasta and cook according to the package directions until al dente. Drain well and set aside.

2. **To make the sauce:** Return the pasta pot to medium-high heat and add the potato, onion, peppers, garlic, cashews, and vegetable broth and season with salt. Bring to a boil. Reduce the heat to maintain a simmer, cover the pot, and cook for about 12 minutes until the vegetables are tender. Remove from the heat and carefully transfer the vegetable mixture to a high-speed blender. Add the milk, nutritional yeast, miso, cumin, and turmeric and blend until smooth. Transfer the mixture back to the pot and cook over medium-low heat, stirring frequently, to thicken, about 5 minutes. Do not let the sauce burn. It should be thick, but pourable.

3. Stir in the salsa and lemon juice. Taste and adjust the seasoning, as needed.

4. Return the pasta to the pot and gently stir to combine with the sauce. Cook over low heat until hot, about 10 minutes. Transfer to a large casserole dish.

5. **To finish:** Sprinkle with the crushed tortilla chips. Top with diced tomato and avocado and serve.

Makes 4 to 6 servings

CREAMY CURRY MAC

Pasta

16 ounces (454 g) elbow macaroni, or
    other small pasta
2 cups (260 g) frozen peas

Sauce

1 tablespoon (15 ml) neutral
    vegetable oil
⅓ cup (55 g) minced onion
2 garlic cloves, minced
1 tablespoon (6 g) garam masala
1 teaspoon grated peeled fresh ginger
1 teaspoon ground coriander
1 teaspoon salt
¼ teaspoon ground black pepper
¼ teaspoon ground turmeric
¼ teaspoon cayenne
1 (14.5-ounce, or 410 g) can diced
    tomatoes, undrained
⅓ cup (47 g) unsalted raw cashews,
    soaked in hot water for 30 minutes,
    drained
2 tablespoons (7.5 g) nutritional yeast
1 (13-ounce, or 385 ml) can
    coconut milk
2 tablespoons (2 g) minced
    fresh cilantro

The first time I combined this creamy curry saucy with pasta, I wondered what took me so long. If you love both the flavor of curry and the texture of mac uncheese, this one's for you.

1. **To make the pasta:** Bring a large pot of salted water to a boil over high heat. Add the pasta and cook according to the package directions until al dente. Add the peas to the pasta. Drain the pasta and peas well and set aside.

2. **To make the sauce:** In a large saucepan over medium heat, heat the vegetable oil.

3. Add the onion and garlic, and cook, stirring, for 1 minute. Stir in the garam masala, ginger, coriander, salt, black pepper, turmeric, and cayenne. Cook for 2 minutes more.

4. Stir in the tomatoes and their juice and the cashews. Bring the mixture just to a boil. Reduce the heat to maintain a simmer and cook for 5 to 7 minutes. Cool slightly, then carefully transfer to a high-speed blender. Add the nutritional yeast and coconut milk and blend until smooth. Return the sauce to the saucepan over low heat.

5. Add the macaroni and peas and cook, stirring, for a few minutes to mix well and heat through. Taste and adjust the seasoning, as needed.

6. Transfer to a large casserole dish and serve garnished with the cilantro.

Makes 4 to 6 servings

NOODLE KUGEL

Olive oil or nonstick cooking oil spray, for preparing the baking dish

16 ounces (454 g) egg-free noodles, or fettucine noodles, broken in half

4 cups (560 g) diced butternut squash, or sweet potato

¾ cup (105 g) unsalted raw cashews

½ cup (80 g) chopped onion

1 small garlic clove, crushed

1½ cups (360 ml) plain unsweetened nondairy milk, plus more as needed

2 tablespoons (30 ml) fresh lemon juice

1 teaspoon salt

1 cup (56 g) crispy fried onions (see note), or crushed corn flakes

Look for egg-free noodles to make this more kugel-like (although it's still tasty made with fettucine). For a heartier casserole, add cooked chopped broccoli or spinach. I especially like it topped with French-fried onions or crushed corn flakes.

1. Preheat the oven to 350°F (180°C). Lightly coat a large baking dish with olive oil or cooking oil spray. Set aside.

2. Bring a large pot of salted water to a boil over high heat. Add the pasta and cook according to the package directions until al dente. Drain well and return it to the pot.

3. Bring a large saucepan of water to a boil over high heat. Add the squash, cashews, onion, and garlic and cook for about 10 minutes until the vegetables are tender. Drain and transfer to a high-speed blender.

4. Add the milk, lemon juice, and salt and blend until smooth. If the sauce is too thick, add a little more milk. Pour the sauce over the cooked pasta and toss to combine. Transfer the pasta to the prepared baking dish, smoothing the top.

5. Sprinkle the top with the onions and bake for 20 minutes to warm through.

Makes 4 to 6 servings

NOTE

Look for a brand of crispy fried onions made without palm oil, such as Market Pantry French-Fried Onions (Target brand) or Archer Farms Crispy Onion Strings.

BAJAN MACARONI PIE

Nonstick cooking oil spray, for
preparing the baking dish

16 ounces (454 g) penne, or other
small tubular pasta

4 scallions, white and green parts,
finely chopped

1 small green bell pepper, chopped

½ cup (30 g) chopped fresh parsley

1 garlic clove, minced

¼ cup (56 g) vegan mayonnaise

2 tablespoons (30 g) ketchup

1½ tablespoons (17 g) prepared
yellow mustard

1½ teaspoons paprika

1 teaspoon minced fresh thyme

¼ teaspoon chipotle chili powder, plus
more as needed

⅛ teaspoon ground cloves

2 cups (450 g) Cheddary Sauce (page
103) or (168 g) shredded vegan
cheddar cheese, divided

Salt, to taste

Ground black pepper, to taste

¼ cup (13 g) Toasted Panko Crumbs
(page 25)

In Barbados, the locals enjoy a macaroni pie reminiscent of a creamy macaroni salad one would find in the United States, but with a little extra kick. A short tubular pasta is traditional.

1. Preheat the oven to 350°F (180°C). Lightly coat a 3-quart (2.8 L) baking dish with cooking spray and set aside.

2. Bring a large pot of salted water to a boil over high heat. Add the pasta and cook according to the package directions until al dente. Drain well and transfer to a large bowl.

3. To the pasta, add the scallions, bell pepper, parsley, garlic, mayonnaise, ketchup, mustard, paprika, thyme, chipotle powder, cloves, and 1 cup (225 g) of Cheddary Sauce. Season with salt and pepper. Stir well to combine and transfer the mixture to the prepared baking dish, spreading it evenly.

4. Spread the remaining 1 cup (225 g) of Cheddary Sauce on top and sprinkle with the toasted panko. Bake for 20 minutes, or until hot.

Makes 4 to 6 servings

BERBERE-SPICED MAC UNCHEESE

Nonstick cooking spray, for preparing the baking dish

Pasta

16 ounces (454 g) elbow macaroni, or other small pasta

Sauce

¾ cup (105 g) unsalted raw cashews, soaked in boiling water for 30 minutes, drained

3½ cups (840 ml) water, divided

½ cup (30 g) nutritional yeast

1 tablespoon (9 g) Berbere Spice Blend (page 63) or store-bought

1 teaspoon salt, plus more as needed

¾ teaspoon onion powder

½ teaspoon garlic powder

¼ teaspoon ground turmeric

Freshly ground black pepper, to taste

½ cup (62 g) all-purpose flour

3 tablespoons (45 ml) olive oil

¾ cup (98 g) frozen green peas, thawed

Mild paprika, for garnish

Wake up your taste buds with this exotic mac uncheese seasoned with berbere, an Ethiopian spice blend. Make your own berbere (recipe opposite) or buy a ready-made blend such as those made by Penzey's or Frontier brand.

1. Preheat the oven to 350°F (180°C). Coat a 3½-quart (3.3 L) baking dish with cooking spray. Set aside.

2. **To make the pasta:** Bring a large pot of salted water to a boil over high heat. Add the pasta and cook according to the package directions until al dente. Drain well and transfer to the prepared baking dish.

3. **To make the sauce:** In a high-speed blender, combine the cashews, 3 cups (720 ml) of water, nutritional yeast, Berbere Spice Blend, salt, onion powder, garlic powder, and turmeric and season with pepper. Blend until completely smooth, stopping to scrape down the sides, as needed.

4. In a medium saucepan over medium-low heat, toast the flour, stirring occasionally, until slightly fragrant, about 1 minute.

5. Stir in the olive oil. Increase the heat to medium and cook the flour, stirring constantly, until it darkens a bit, about 1 minute.

6. Whisking constantly, slowly add the cashew mixture and cook until it becomes a thick sauce, about 3 minutes. Remove from the heat. Stir in up to ½ cup (120 ml) of the remaining water if the sauce is too thick. Add the sauce and peas to the pasta, stir to combine, and smooth the top.

7. Sprinkle with paprika, cover the baking dish with aluminum foil, and bake for 20 minutes, or until hot.

Makes 4 to 6 servings

BERBERE SPICE BLEND

2 tablespoons (11 g) ground cayenne
2 tablespoons (17 g) sweet paprika
2 teaspoons salt
1 teaspoon ground coriander
½ teaspoon ground ginger
½ teaspoon ground fenugreek seed
½ teaspoon ground black pepper
¼ teaspoon ground cardamom
¼ teaspoon ground cumin
¼ teaspoon ground turmeric
¼ teaspoon ground cinnamon
¼ teaspoon ground nutmeg
¼ teaspoon ground allspice
⅛ teaspoon ground cloves

This recipe keeps it simple by using already ground spices.

In a small bowl, combine all the ingredients and stir well to mix. Store in a tightly sealed container in a cool place.

Makes about ⅓ cup (about 50 g)

PASTITSIO

Nonstick cooking oil spray, for preparing the baking dish

16 ounces (454 g) penne, or other small tubular pasta

1 tablespoon (15 ml) olive oil

1 medium onion, chopped

2 garlic cloves, minced

2 cups (164 g) chopped peeled eggplant

1½ cups (105 g) chopped mushrooms

⅓ cup (80 ml) dry red wine

½ teaspoon dried oregano

1 (24-ounce, or 675 g) jar of marinara sauce

1 teaspoon salt, divided

⅛ teaspoon ground cinnamon

⅓ cup (75 g) vegan butter, diced

½ cup (62 g) all-purpose flour

¼ teaspoon ground black pepper

3½ cups (840 ml) plain unsweetened nondairy milk

Chopped mushrooms and eggplant in tomato sauce replace the ground meat in this Greek iteration of mac and cheese. The traditional dish is made with bucatini, but any tubular pasta will work—I like it with penne. If you're not a fan of eggplant, substitute chopped peeled zucchini, or simply use more mushrooms.

1. Coat a 9 × 13-inch (23 × 33 cm) baking dish with cooking oil spray. Set aside.

2. Bring a large pot of salted water to a boil over high heat. Add the pasta and cook according to the package directions until al dente. Drain well and transfer to the prepared baking dish.

3. Preheat the oven to 350°F (180°C).

4. In a saucepan over medium heat, heat the olive oil. Add the onion and cook until softened, about 5 minutes. Add the garlic, eggplant, and mushrooms, and cook for 5 minutes more, or until the eggplant is tender. Stir in the wine and oregano.

5. Stir in the marinara sauce, ½ teaspoon of salt, and the cinnamon. Cook until heated through. Spoon the sauce mixture over the pasta, gently stirring to combine.

6. Rinse out the saucepan and return it to medium heat. Add the butter to melt. Stir in the flour, remaining ½ teaspoon of salt, and the pepper, stirring until smooth.

7. Stirring constantly, gradually add the milk. Bring to a boil. Reduce the heat to maintain a simmer and cook, stirring, for 1 minute, or until thickened. Pour the sauce over the pasta mixture. Cover the baking dish with aluminum foil and bake for 20 minutes.

8. Uncover and bake for 15 minutes longer or until golden.

Makes 4 to 6 servings

MAC AND CREOLE

1 tablespoon (15 ml) olive oil, or ¼ cup (60 ml) water
1 sweet yellow onion, chopped
1 bell pepper (any color), chopped
1 celery stalk, chopped
1 small jalapeño pepper, seeded and minced
Salt, to taste
Ground black pepper, to taste
16 ounces (454 g) small pasta shells
⅓ cup (75 g) vegan butter
⅓ cup (41 g) unbleached all-purpose flour
⅓ cup (20 g) nutritional yeast
1 to 2 tablespoons (12 to 24 g) Creole spice blend, such as Tony Chachere's Creole Seasoning
1 teaspoon smoked paprika
½ teaspoon prepared yellow mustard
⅛ teaspoon cayenne pepper
2 cups (480 ml) plain unsweetened nondairy milk
1½ cups (168 g) shredded vegan cheddar, or 2 cups (450 g) Cheddary Sauce (page 103)
½ cup (55 g) toasted chopped pecans
Louisiana hot sauce, for serving

From a sauté of the vegetable trinity to a roux-based sauce and a zesty Creole spice blend, this mac uncheese is a taste of Louisiana. If you want to up the ante, fold in some sliced cooked vegan andouille sausage and sliced cooked okra.

1. In a skillet over medium heat, heat the olive oil. Add the onion, bell pepper, celery, and jalapeno and season with salt and black pepper. Cook, stirring frequently, until the vegetables are tender, about 12 minutes. Set aside.

2. Bring a large pot of salted water to a boil over high heat. Add the pasta and cook according to the package directions until al dente. Drain well and return it to the pot.

3. In a saucepan over medium heat, melt the butter. Stir in the flour, nutritional yeast, Creole spice blend, paprika, mustard, and cayenne.

4. Stirring constantly, add the milk, and stir until smooth. Add the cheddar, stirring until it melts.

5. Add the cooked vegetables to the cooked pasta. Pour the cheese sauce on top and gently stir to combine. Place the pot over medium heat and cook, stirring gently, until hot. Taste and season with salt and pepper, as needed. Transfer the pasta mixture to a 9 × 13-inch (23 × 33 cm) baking dish.

6. Sprinkle the pecans evenly over the top. Serve hot with hot sauce on the side.

Makes 4 to 6 servings

CHAPTER 3

Mac and Veggies

Sometimes the addition of veggies to a mac and cheese dish can be almost an afterthought. Not so with the recipes in this chapter where the vegetables are the stars of the show. The Spinach-Artichoke Mac and Cheese (page 70) is reminiscent of the eponymous dip, while Asparagus Mac and Hollandaise (page 81) brings a touch of elegance to the comfort food casserole.

ROASTED BUTTERNUT MAC UNCHEESE

3 cups (420 g) diced butternut squash
Olive oil
Salt, to taste
Ground black pepper, to taste
16 ounces (454 g) elbow macaroni or
other bite-size pasta
½ cup (70 g) unsalted raw cashews,
soaked overnight and drained
2 cups (480 ml) plain unsweetened
almond milk, divided
2 tablespoons (30 ml) freshly
squeezed lemon juice
1 teaspoon Dijon mustard
½ cup (30 g) nutritional yeast
1 teaspoon salt
1 teaspoon onion powder
½ teaspoon garlic powder
½ teaspoon smoked paprika
¼ teaspoon ground black pepper
¼ cup (13 g) Toasted Panko Crumbs
(page 25), for garnish
3 tablespoons (30 g) roasted hulled
pumpkin seeds (pepitas), for garnish

Butternut squash and cashews combine to make the creamy sauce for this mac uncheese. For a variation, add cooked green vegetables, such as broccoli or peas. To make this gluten free, use gluten-free pasta and bread crumbs.

1. Preheat the oven to 425°F (220°C). Arrange the squash on a rimmed baking pan lined with parchment paper. Drizzle or spray with olive oil, then season with salt and pepper. Roast until tender, stirring occasionally, about 25 minutes. Remove from the oven and set aside.

2. Cook the macaroni in a pot of boiling salted water until it is al dente. Drain and return to the pot.

3. In a high-speed blender, combine the cashews and 1 cup (240 ml) of the almond milk and process until smooth. Add the roasted squash, lemon juice, mustard, nutritional yeast, 1 teaspoon salt, onion powder, garlic powder, paprika, ¼ teaspoon black pepper, and the remaining almond milk and blend until smooth and creamy.

4. Add the sauce to the pot with the macaroni and stir to combine. Taste and adjust the seasoning, if needed. Heat over low heat for a few minutes, if needed. To serve, transfer to a large serving bowl and serve hot sprinkled with the Toasted Panko Crumbs and pumpkin seeds.

Makes 4 to 6 servings

CHEESY SPAGHETTI SQUASH MAC

1 large spaghetti squash, seeded and cut into 8 pieces

¼ cup (60 ml) olive oil, plus more for preparing the baking dish and drizzling

Salt, to taste

Ground black pepper, to taste

1 yellow onion, minced

2 garlic cloves, minced

¼ cup (31 g) all-purpose flour

2 cups (480 ml) plain unsweetened nondairy milk

1 cup (240 ml) vegetable broth

⅓ cup (20 g) nutritional yeast

1 teaspoon white miso paste

1 tablespoon (15 ml) fresh lemon juice

1½ cups (195 g) frozen peas

1 cup (150 g) halved grape tomatoes

1 cup (230 g) Cheddary Sauce (page 103), or (112 g) shredded vegan cheddar cheese

¾ cup (170 g) chopped Tempeh Bacon (page 87)

This is a great way to enjoy mac uncheese without the macaroni and a tasty way to serve spaghetti squash.

1. Preheat the oven to 400°F (200°C). Line a baking sheet with parchment paper. Coat a 3-quart (2.8 L) baking dish with olive oil. Set aside.

2. Arrange the squash pieces on the prepared sheet, drizzle with olive oil, and season with salt and pepper. Bake for 45 minutes, or until tender. Remove and let cool slightly. Scrape out the squash strands with a fork and set aside.

3. Lower the oven temperature to 350°F (180°C).

4. In a large saucepan over medium heat, heat the olive oil.

5. Add the onion and cook for 5 minutes, or until soft. Add the garlic and cook, stirring, for 1 minute more.

6. Add the flour and cook, whisking constantly, for 3 minutes.

7. Increase the heat slightly and add the milk and vegetable broth. Cook, whisking, until the mixture becomes thick, about 10 minutes. Remove from the heat and whisk in the nutritional yeast and miso until blended.

8. Add the lemon juice, peas, tomatoes, and spaghetti squash strands and season with salt and pepper. Toss well to combine. Transfer to the prepared baking dish.

9. Drizzle the Cheddary Sauce over top, or sprinkle with the cheese, and scatter the bacon around. Bake, uncovered, until golden brown, about 20 minutes. Serve immediately.

Makes 4 to 6 servings

SPINACH-ARTICHOKE MAC AND CHEESE

Olive oil or vegan butter, for preparing the baking dish

16 ounces (454 g) rotini, or other bite-size pasta

2 cups (60 g) chopped baby spinach

1 pound (454 g) firm silken tofu, well drained

1 cup (240 ml) vegetable broth

¼ cup (15 g) nutritional yeast

2 tablespoons (30 ml) dry white wine

1 tablespoon (15 ml) fresh lemon juice

1 tablespoon (8 g) cornstarch

1 teaspoon garlic powder

½ teaspoon dried basil

Salt, to taste

Ground black pepper, to taste

1 (12-ounce, or 340 g) jar marinated artichoke hearts, drained and coarsely chopped

3 scallions, white and green parts, minced

⅓ cup (50 g) quartered cherry or grape tomatoes

¼ cup (40 g) Kalamata olives, pitted and coarsely chopped

2 tablespoons (5 g) chopped fresh basil or (8 g) parsley

¼ cup (13 g) Toasted Panko Crumbs (page 25), optional

Inspired by the classic spinach-artichoke dip, this mac uncheese also features Kalamata olives, cherry tomatoes, and fresh basil. It's a favorite at parties.

1. Preheat the oven to 375°F (190°C). Lightly coat a 3½- to 4-quart (3.3 to 3.8 L) baking dish with olive oil or vegan butter. Set aside.

2. Bring a large pot of salted water to a boil over high heat. Add the pasta and cook according to the package directions until al dente. Stir in the spinach, drain, and return the mixture to the pot.

3. In a food processor or blender, combine the tofu, vegetable broth, nutritional yeast, wine, lemon juice, cornstarch, garlic powder, and dried basil and season with salt and pepper. Process until smooth and well blended. Add the tofu mixture to the cooked pasta.

4. Add the artichoke hearts, scallions, tomatoes, olives, and fresh basil. Gently stir to combine. Spread the mixture evenly into the prepared baking dish. Sprinkle with the panko, if using. Loosely cover and bake until hot, about 20 minutes. Serve hot.

Makes 4 to 6 servings

NOTE

For even richer flavor, substitute 8 ounces (227 g) vegan cream cheese for half of the tofu.

RUTABAGA MAC AND GREENS

Pasta

16 ounces (454 g) elbow macaroni, or
  other small pasta
6 cups (180 g) chopped spinach, chard,
  or other dark leafy greens

Sauce

12 ounces (340 g) rutabaga, peeled
  and cut into 1-inch (2.5 cm) dice
1 (8-ounce, or 225 g) russet potato,
  peeled and cut into 1-inch
  (2.5 cm) dice
½ cup (80 g) chopped yellow onion
⅔ cup (40 g) nutritional yeast
½ cup (120 ml) white wine
2 tablespoons (30 ml) apple
  cider vinegar
½ teaspoon prepared yellow mustard
2 tablespoons (34 g) white miso paste
1 tablespoon (15 ml) fresh lemon juice
Salt, to taste

Topping

½ cup (30 g) crushed pretzels
Cracked black pepper, to taste

The sauce for this mac uncheese was inspired by the incomparable rutabaga fondue served at Rich Landau's amazing restaurants—Vedge in Philadelphia and Fancy Radish in Washington D.C.

1. **To make the pasta:** Bring a large pot of salted water to a boil over high heat. Add the pasta and cook according to the package directions until al dente. About 2 minutes before the pasta is done, stir in the greens. Drain the pasta and greens well and return them to the pot. Set aside.

2. **To make the sauce:** Bring a medium pot of salted water to boil over high heat. Add the rutabaga and cook for 10 minutes, or until it can be pierced with a fork.

3. Add the potato and onion and cook for 10 minutes more, or until soft. Reserve 1½ cups (360 ml) of the cooking water. Drain the vegetables and return them to the pot.

4. Stir in the nutritional yeast, wine, vinegar, mustard, and reserved cooking water. Place the pot over high heat and bring to a boil. Cook for 1 minute. Reduce the heat to maintain a simmer.

5. Stir in the miso and lemon juice and carefully transfer the sauce mixture to a blender or food processor. Blend until smooth and creamy. Taste and add salt, as needed. Pour the sauce onto the pasta and greens and stir to combine. Place the pot over low heat and cook until well combined and heated through. Transfer to a serving dish.

6. **To finish:** Sprinkle with crushed pretzels and pepper. Serve hot.

Makes 4 to 6 servings

CHEESY BROCCOLI MAC

Sauce

1½ cups (210 g) unsalted raw cashews, soaked in boiling water for 30 minutes and drained

3 garlic cloves, peeled

2 tablespoons (30 ml) fresh lemon juice

1 teaspoon salt

1 teaspoon white miso paste

⅓ cup (20 g) nutritional yeast

3 cups (720 ml) plain unsweetened nondairy milk

Pasta

16 ounces (454 g) penne, or other small pasta

3 cups (213 g) small broccoli florets

Topping

½ cup (25 g) Toasted Panko Crumbs (page 25), or your favorite topping (optional)

Cracked black pepper, to taste

Broccoli has a natural affinity with cheesy sauces, so it's no wonder it's terrific in mac uncheese.

1. **To make the sauce:** In a high-speed blender, combine the cashews, garlic, lemon juice, salt, miso, nutritional yeast, and milk. Blend until smooth and creamy, stopping to scrape down the sides, as needed. Set aside.

2. **To make the pasta:** Bring a large pot of salted water to a boil over high heat. Add the pasta and cook according to the package directions until al dente. During the last 4 minutes of cooking time, add the broccoli florets to the pot. Drain the pasta and broccoli and return them to the pot.

3. Pour in the sauce and stir to combine. Place the pot over low heat and cook until hot. Taste and adjust the seasoning, as needed.

4. **To finish:** Transfer the pasta to a serving dish and sprinkle with the Toasted Panko Crumbs (if using) and pepper.

Makes 4 to 6 servings

BUFFALO CAULIFLOWER MAC

Sauce
1 large russet potato, cut into 1-inch (2.5 cm) chunks
1 large carrot, cut into 1-inch (2.5 cm) chunks
2½ cups (600 ml) vegetable broth
⅔ cup (40 g) nutritional yeast
2 tablespoons (30 ml) tamari
½ teaspoon onion powder
½ teaspoon garlic powder
Salt, to taste

Cauliflower
1 head of cauliflower, cored and cut into bite-size pieces
Olive oil cooking spray
1 teaspoon garlic powder
Salt, to taste
⅓ cup (80 ml) hot pepper sauce, preferably Frank's RedHot
4 tablespoons (56 g) vegan butter, melted
1 tablespoon (15 ml) apple cider vinegar
1 teaspoon paprika

Pasta
16 ounces (454 g) elbow macaroni, or other small pasta

Buffalo cauliflower has been making the rounds, so it should come as no surprise that it turns up in a mac uncheese. The cheesy, saucy macaroni is a perfect foil for the spicy hot cauliflower.

1. **To make the sauce:** In a medium saucepan over medium-high heat, combine the potato, carrot, and vegetable broth. Bring to a boil and cook for 15 to 20 minutes, or until the vegetables are tender when pierced with a fork. Carefully transfer the mixture to a blender or food processor. Add the nutritional yeast, tamari, onion powder, and garlic powder and season with salt. Blend until smooth. Set aside.

2. Preheat the oven to 400°F (200°C). Line a baking sheet with parchment paper.

3. **To make the cauliflower:** Arrange the cauliflower in a single layer on the prepared sheet. Spray the cauliflower with cooking spray and sprinkle with the garlic powder and salt. Roast for 20 minutes or until softened. Transfer to a large bowl and add the hot sauce, butter, vinegar, and paprika. Stir well to coat. Return the cauliflower to the baking sheet (you may want to use a new sheet of parchment) and arrange it in a single layer. Bake for 10 minutes more.

4. **To make the pasta:** Bring a large pot of salted water to a boil over high heat. Add the pasta and cook according to the package directions until al dente. Drain well and return it to the pot.

5. Stir in the sauce and place the pot over low heat. Cook for a few minutes to heat through.

6. Add the buffalo cauliflower and gently stir to combine. Serve hot.

Makes 4 to 6 servings

ARUGULA PESTO MAC UNCHEESE

Pasta

16 ounces (454 g) ziti, or other
   small pasta

Sauce

4 tablespoons (56 g) vegan butter

⅓ cup (41 g) unbleached
   all-purpose flour

3 cups (720 ml) plain unsweetened
   nondairy milk, or more

1 teaspoon salt

1 teaspoon white miso paste

1 teaspoon almond butter

1 teaspoon garlic powder

½ teaspoon onion powder

½ teaspoon ground turmeric

¼ teaspoon ground black pepper

1 teaspoon fresh lemon juice

½ cup (30 g) nutritional yeast

⅓ cup (62 g) Arugula Pesto
   (page 80), or more

1 cup (180 g) chopped fresh tomatoes

½ cup (64 g) Nut Parm (page 55,
   optional)

½ cup (20 g) chopped fresh basil

A heady arugula pesto adds an aromatic note to this mac uncheese.
Chopped fresh tomatoes are added for color and flavor.

1. **To make the pasta:** Bring a large pot of salted water to a boil over high
   heat. Add the pasta and cook according to the package directions until
   just al dente. Drain the pasta well and return it to the pot. Set aside.

2. **To make the sauce:** In a saucepan over medium heat, melt the butter.
   Whisk in the flour and cook for about 1 minute. Whisk in the milk, salt,
   miso, almond butter, garlic powder, onion powder, turmeric, and pepper.
   Cook, whisking, for 1 to 2 minutes to blend.

3. Whisk in the lemon juice, nutritional yeast, and Arugula Pesto. Add more
   milk or pesto to achieve desired flavor and consistency. Pour the sauce
   over the pasta.

4. Add the tomatoes and toss to combine. Place the pot over low heat and
   cook for 2 minutes, or until the pasta is hot. Transfer to a serving dish
   and sprinkle with the Nut Parm (if using) and basil.

Makes 4 to 6 servings

ARUGULA PESTO

3 garlic cloves, crushed
¼ cup (30 g) toasted walnut pieces
½ teaspoon salt
2 cups (40 g) coarsely
   chopped arugula
½ cup (20 g) fresh basil leaves
2 tablespoons (30 ml) olive oil
1 tablespoon (15 ml) fresh lemon juice
¼ teaspoon freshly ground
   black pepper
Warm water, as needed

Arugula makes a flavorful pesto that can also be used on pizza or in salads, dressings, or soups. Portion and freeze any leftover pesto for later use.

1. In a food processor, combine the garlic, walnuts, and salt and process to a paste.

2. Add the arugula, basil, olive oil, lemon juice, and pepper and process to a paste.

3. If needed, add a little warm water, 1 tablespoon (15 ml) at a time, to reach the desired consistency. If not using right away, transfer to a container with a tight-fitting lid, cover, and refrigerate until needed.

Makes about 1½ cups (about 150 g)

ASPARAGUS MAC AND HOLLANDAISE

Hollandaise Sauce

3 ripe yellow tomatoes, diced
2 yellow bell peppers, diced
1 tablespoon (15 ml) olive oil
Salt, to taste
2 tablespoons (28 g) vegan butter
1½ tablespoons (23 ml) fresh
    lemon juice
¼ teaspoon prepared yellow mustard
Pinch ground turmeric

Pasta and Asparagus

16 ounces (454 g) penne, or other
    small pasta
1 bunch of asparagus, cut into
    1½-inch (3.5 cm) pieces
    (2½ cups, or about 312 g)
4 tablespoons (56 g) vegan butter
¼ cup (31 g) all-purpose flour
2 cups (480 ml) plain unsweetened
    nondairy milk
1 cup (240 ml) vegetable broth
⅓ cup (20 g) nutritional yeast
2 tablespoons (30 ml) fresh
    lemon juice
½ teaspoon ground turmeric
Salt, to taste
½ cup (68 g) toasted pine
    nuts, crushed

The creamy hollandaise sauce complements the asparagus beautifully and gives this mac uncheese a touch of elegance that makes it ideal for a Sunday brunch or a Saturday night dinner party.

1. Preheat the oven to 400°F (200°C). Line a baking sheet with parchment paper. Set aside.

2. **To make the hollandaise sauce:** In a large bowl, combine the tomatoes and bell peppers. Drizzle the olive oil over the vegetables and toss to coat. Arrange the bell pepper and tomatoes on the prepared sheet and season with salt. Roast for 20 minutes. Flip and roast for 10 minutes more. Transfer the vegetables to a blender or food processor.

3. Add the butter, lemon juice, mustard, and turmeric and blend until smooth. Set aside and keep warm.

4. **To make the pasta and asparagus:** Bring a large pot of salted water to a boil over high heat. Add the pasta and cook according to the package directions until al dente. About 4 minutes before the pasta is done, stir in the asparagus. Drain the cooked pasta and asparagus and return them to the pot. Set aside.

5. In a saucepan over medium heat, melt the butter. Add the flour and cook, whisking constantly, for 2 to 3 minutes.

6. Still whisking constantly, pour in the milk and vegetable broth. Cook, whisking, until it starts to thicken, about 4 minutes. Remove from the heat.

7. Stir in the nutritional yeast, lemon juice, and turmeric and season with salt. Pour the sauce over the pasta and asparagus, stirring to coat. Transfer to a large serving dish and drizzle the reserved hollandaise on top.

8. Sprinkle with the toasted pine nuts and serve hot.

Makes 4 to 6 servings

SMOKY MAC AND PEAS WITH MUSHROOM BACON

Pasta

16 ounces (454 g) radiatore, or other
   small pasta

Sauce

1½ cups (165 g) diced peeled
   sweet potato
½ cup (80 g) chopped onion
½ cup (70 g) unsalted raw cashews
1½ cups (360 ml) canned full-fat
   coconut milk
¼ cup (15 g) nutritional yeast
1 tablespoon (15 ml) fresh lemon juice
1½ teaspoons Dijon mustard
1 teaspoon smoked paprika
½ teaspoon salt
¼ teaspoon onion powder
¼ teaspoon ground turmeric
¼ teaspoon ground black pepper
1 cup (130 g) frozen green peas,
   thawed
1 recipe Mushroom Bacon (page 83)

Sweet potatoes and coconut milk set the stage for this flavor-packed mac uncheese. The sweet pop of green peas and smoky-rich mushroom bacon send it off the charts.

1. **To make the pasta:** Bring a large pot of salted water to a boil over high heat. Add the pasta and cook according to the package directions until al dente. Drain well and return it to the pot. Set aside.

2. **To make the sauce:** In a saucepan, combine the sweet potato, onion, and cashews with enough water to cover. Place the pan over high heat and bring to a boil. Reduce the heat to maintain a simmer and cook until the vegetables are soft, about 12 minutes. Reserve 1 cup (240 ml) of the cooking water. Drain the vegetables and cashews and transfer to a high-speed blender. Add the reserved cooking water and blend until smooth.

3. Add the coconut milk, nutritional yeast, lemon juice, mustard, paprika, salt, onion powder, turmeric, and pepper. Blend until completely smooth, stopping to scrape down the sides, as needed. Add more coconut milk or water if the sauce is too thick. Adjust the seasonings, if needed. Add the sauce to the cooked pasta.

4. Stir in the peas and 1 cup (230 g) of the mushroom bacon and toss to combine. Place the pot over low heat and cook until heated through. Transfer to a large serving dish and sprinkle the top with the remaining mushroom bacon. Serve hot.

Makes 4 to 6 servings

MUSHROOM BACON

Nonstick cooking oil spray
8 ounces (225 g) shiitake mushroom
 caps, thinly sliced
2 tablespoons (30 ml) grapeseed oil,
 divided
Salt, to taste
Ground black pepper, to taste
1 tablespoon (15 ml) tamari
1 tablespoon (20 g) pure maple syrup
1 teaspoon liquid smoke
¼ teaspoon garlic powder
¼ teaspoon smoked paprika
¼ teaspoon light brown sugar

Slices of shiitake mushrooms take on the smoky goodness of bacon. In addition to using in Smoky Mac and Peas with Mushroom Bacon (page 82), try them on salads, tossed with roasted vegetables, or in a tofu scramble.

1. Preheat the oven to 350°F (180°C). Line a rimmed baking sheet with parchment paper and spray it with cooking spray. Set aside.

2. In a medium bowl, combine the sliced mushrooms and 1 tablespoon (15 ml) of grapeseed oil. Toss to coat. Spread the mushrooms on the prepared sheet in a single layer. Lightly season with salt and pepper. Bake for 15 minutes. Using a thin metal spatula, carefully flip the mushroom slices. Bake for 10 to 15 minutes more, until nicely browned and crisp on the edges.

3. In a shallow bowl, stir together the tamari, maple syrup, liquid smoke, garlic powder, paprika, brown sugar, and remaining 1 tablespoon (15 ml) of grapeseed oil. Remove the mushrooms from the oven and add them to the bowl, gently tossing to coat with the marinade. Return the mushrooms to the baking sheet in a single layer and bake for about 5 minutes more, or until nicely glazed.

Makes about 1½ cups (345 g)

BRUSSELS AND BACON CHEESY MAC

Nonstick cooking oil spray

Pasta

16 ounces (454 g) elbow macaroni, or
  other small pasta

Brussels Sprouts

1 pound (454 g) Brussels sprouts,
  trimmed and halved or quartered
  lengthwise (depending on size)
1 tablespoon (15 ml) olive oil
Salt, to taste

Sauce

2 cups (480 ml) water
1 large russet potato, peeled and diced
1 small carrot, chopped
½ of a small yellow onion, chopped
2 garlic cloves, smashed
¾ cup (105 g) unsalted raw cashews
½ teaspoon salt
1 cup (240 ml) unsweetened
  nondairy milk
½ cup (30 g) nutritional yeast
2 tablespoons (28 g) vegan butter
1½ tablespoons (23 ml) fresh
  lemon juice
½ teaspoon prepared yellow mustard
¼ teaspoon ground black pepper
¼ teaspoon ground turmeric
¼ teaspoon smoked paprika
4 to 6 slices Tempeh Bacon (page 87),
  cooked and finely chopped

Roasted Brussels sprouts and smoky Tempeh Bacon team up with creamy, cheesy pasta for a great combination of flavors and textures. Small Brussels sprouts only need to be halved lengthwise, while larger ones should be quartered.

1. Preheat the oven to 425°F (220°C). Line a large baking sheet with parchment paper. Coat a 3½- to 4-quart (3.3 to 3.8 L) baking dish with cooking spray. Set aside.

2. **To make the pasta:** Bring a large pot of salted water to a boil over high heat. Add the pasta and cook according to the package directions until al dente. Drain well and set aside.

3. **To make the Brussels sprouts:** In a medium bowl, combine the Brussels sprouts and olive oil and season with salt. Toss to coat. Arrange the vegetables in a single layer on the prepared sheet and bake for 15 to 20 minutes, or until softened and lightly browned. Reduce the oven temperature to 375°F (190°C).

4. **To make the sauce:** In the now-empty pasta pot, combine the water, potato, carrot, onion, garlic, cashews, and ½ teaspoon of salt. Place the pot over high heat and bring to a boil. Reduce the heat to maintain a simmer, cover the pot, and cook for 10 to 15 minutes until the vegetables are soft. Carefully transfer the contents of the pot to a high-speed blender or food processor.

5. Add the milk, nutritional yeast, butter, lemon juice, mustard, pepper, turmeric, and paprika. Blend until completely smooth, stopping to scrape down the sides, as needed.

6. Return the pasta to the pot and pour the sauce over it. Add the roasted Brussels sprouts and gently stir to combine. Transfer the mixture to the prepared baking dish and sprinkle the top with the chopped bacon. Bake for 20 minutes.

Makes 4 to 6 servings

TEMPEH BACON

1 (8-ounce, or 225 g) package tempeh, cut lengthwise into thin strips
3 tablespoons (45 ml) tamari
3 tablespoons (60 g) pure maple syrup, or agave syrup
2 tablespoons (30 ml) apple cider vinegar
2 tablespoons (30 ml) water
1 teaspoon liquid smoke
½ teaspoon smoked paprika
½ teaspoon ground black pepper
2 tablespoons (30 ml) olive oil

In the vegan food world, "bacon" means smoky, salty, savory, crispy, chewy goodness—no animal flesh needed. Best of all, it's high in protein and can be easily cut into thin slices.

1. Arrange the tempeh slices in a shallow baking dish, overlapping slightly, if needed. Set aside.

2. In a small saucepan over medium heat, whisk the tamari, maple syrup, vinegar, water, liquid smoke, paprika, and pepper and cook until hot. Pour the hot mixture over the tempeh slices and set aside for 15 to 20 minutes to allow the tempeh to absorb the marinade.

3. In a large skillet over medium-high heat, heat the olive oil. Working in batches, add the tempeh and cook, turning once, until nicely browned, about 5 minutes. As the tempeh cooks, pour any remaining marinade over it and allow it to evaporate.

Makes 12 to 16 strips

CHEESY PRIMAVERA MAC

Sauce

1 large russet potato, peeled and
  chopped
1 medium carrot, chopped
2 garlic cloves, peeled
½ cup (70 g) unsalted raw cashews
⅓ cup (20 g) nutritional yeast
2 tablespoons (30 ml) olive oil
1½ teaspoons smoked paprika
1 tablespoon (17 g) white miso paste
1 tablespoon (15 ml) fresh lemon juice
Salt, to taste
Ground black pepper, to taste

Pasta and Vegetables

16 ounces (454 g) tricolor rotini, or
  other small pasta
2 cups (142 g) small broccoli florets
3 scallions, white and green parts,
  minced
2 cups (60 g) chopped fresh spinach,
  arugula, or watercress
1 cup (149 g) cherry tomatoes, halved
  or quartered
¼ cup (36 g) roasted hulled sunflower
  seeds, for garnish (optional)
Handful small basil leaves,
  for garnish (optional)

I like to use tricolor rotini in this lovely springtime casserole to mirror the gorgeous colors of the vegetables in the dish.

1. **To make the sauce:** In a saucepan, combine the potato, carrot, garlic, and cashews with enough water to cover. Place the pan over high heat and bring to a boil. Cook until the vegetables are tender, about 10 minutes. Reserve 2 cups (480 ml) of the cooking water. Drain and transfer the cooked vegetables and cashews to a high-speed blender, along with the reserved cooking water.

2. Add the nutritional yeast, olive oil, paprika, miso, and lemon juice and season with salt and pepper. Blend until smooth. Taste and adjust the seasoning, as needed. Set aside.

3. **To make the pasta and vegetables:** Bring a large pot of salted water to a boil over high heat. Add the pasta and cook according to the package directions until al dente. About 5 minutes before the pasta is done, add the broccoli to the pot. Drain the pasta and broccoli and return them to the pot.

4. Place the pot over low heat and add the scallions, spinach, and cherry tomatoes and toss to combine.

5. Pour the sauce over the pasta and vegetables and toss to combine and heat through. Transfer to a large serving dish and serve hot, garnished with sunflower seeds and basil leaves (if using).

Makes 4 to 6 servings

ROASTED VEGETABLE CHEESY MAC

3 plum tomatoes, cored and halved
    lengthwise
1 russet potato, peeled and diced
1 medium carrot, sliced
1 yellow bell pepper, cut into strips
2 garlic cloves, smashed
Salt, to taste
16 ounces (454 g) penne, or other
    small pasta
1 cup (240 ml) water
½ cup (30 g) nutritional yeast
2½ tablespoons (37.5 ml) fresh
    lemon juice
1 teaspoon onion powder
1 teaspoon smoked paprika
½ teaspoon prepared yellow mustard
¼ teaspoon ground turmeric
¼ teaspoon garlic powder
Ground black pepper, to taste
¼ cup (13 g) Toasted Panko Crumbs
    (page 25), or your favorite topping

Roasting the vegetables for this sauce provides a deep, complex flavor to this mac uncheese. Made without oil, nuts, or soy, it can also be made gluten free if you use gluten-free pasta and bread crumbs.

1. Preheat the oven to 425°F (220°C). Line a baking sheet with parchment paper.

2. Spread the tomatoes, potato, carrot, bell pepper, and garlic on the prepared sheet. Season with salt. Roast until soft, about 45 minutes, stirring occasionally. Set aside to cool slightly.

3. While the vegetables roast, bring a large pot of salted water to a boil over high heat. Add the pasta and cook according to the package directions until al dente. Drain well and return to the pot. Set aside.

4. In a blender or food processor, combine the water, nutritional yeast, lemon juice, onion powder, paprika, mustard, turmeric, and garlic powder and season with salt and pepper. Add the roasted vegetables and process until smooth. Add the sauce to the cooked pasta and toss to combine. If needed, place the pot over low heat to heat through. Transfer to a 3½ to 4-quart (3.3 to 3.8 L) serving dish and sprinkle with the Toasted Panko Crumbs. Serve hot.

Makes 4 to 6 servings

MAC AND GIARDINIERA

1 large russet potato, peeled and diced

1 medium carrot, peeled and coarsely chopped

1 medium yellow onion, coarsely chopped

½ cup (70 g) unsalted raw cashews

Salt, to taste

16 ounces (454 g) campanelle, or other small pasta

1 teaspoon garlic powder

1 teaspoon onion powder

¼ cup (15 g) nutritional yeast

1 teaspoon salt

1½ cups (203 g) hot pickled vegetables (giardiniera), drained and coarsely chopped

Jars of hot pickled vegetables known as *giardiniera* are widely available in supermarkets. A mild version is also available for those who prefer it. The zesty flavor of the vegetables brightens the creamy pasta and sauce.

1. **To make the sauce:** Combine the potato, carrot, onion, and cashews in a large pot with enough water to cover. Bring to a boil, salt the water, and reduce the heat to a simmer. Cook for 15 minutes, or until the vegetables are tender. Drain, reserving 2 cups (480 ml) of the cooking water.

2. **To make the pasta:** Using the same pot, bring about 2 quarts (1.9 L) of water to a boil. Salt the water and add the pasta. Cook, stirring occasionally, until the pasta is al dente. Drain and return to the pot.

3. Transfer the cooked vegetable and cashew mixture to a high-speed blender. Add the garlic powder, onion powder, nutritional yeast, 1 teaspoon of salt, and 1 cup (240 ml) of the reserved cooking water. Blend until smooth. Add as much of the remaining cooking water as desired to achieve a smooth sauce.

4. Pour the sauce over the macaroni. Add the pickled vegetables and stir to coat. Serve hot.

Makes 4 to 6 servings

ROASTED GARLIC MAC AND CHEESE

Pasta

16 ounces (454 g) cavatappi, or other
   small pasta

Sauce

¼ cup (60 ml) olive oil

2 garlic cloves, minced

¼ cup (31 g) unbleached all-purpose
   flour

3 cups (720 ml) plain unsweetened
   nondairy milk, plus more as needed

1 head of roasted garlic (see Note)

½ cup (64 g) Nut Parm (page 55),
   divided

⅓ cup (20 g) nutritional yeast

Salt, to taste

Ground black pepper, to taste

¼ cup (13 g) Toasted Panko Crumbs
   (page 25)

½ teaspoon smoked paprika

Garlic lovers will clamor for this mac uncheese made with an entire head of roasted garlic. No worries that it will be too garlicky, as roasting mellows the garlic's flavor.

1. **To make the pasta:** Bring a large pot of salted water to a boil over high heat. Add the pasta and cook according to the package directions until al dente. Drain well and return it to the pot. Set aside.

2. **To make the sauce:** In a large skillet over medium heat, heat the olive oil. Add the minced garlic. Cook, stirring for 1 minute. Stir in the flour.

3. Slowly add the milk, whisking to prevent clumping. Cook for about 5 minutes to blend and thicken slightly, whisking frequently. Transfer the sauce to a blender.

4. Add the roasted garlic, ¼ cup (32 g) of Nut Parm, and nutritional yeast and season with salt and pepper. Blend until smooth. Taste and adjust the seasoning, as needed. Pour the sauce over the cooked pasta and toss to coat. Place the pot over low heat and cook, stirring occasionally, for 2 to 3 minutes, or until the pasta is hot and the sauce thickens slightly. If the sauce is too thick, add a bit more milk. Transfer to a serving dish.

5. Sprinkle the top with the remaining ¼ cup (32 g) of Nut Parm, the Toasted Panko Crumbs, and paprika. Serve hot.

Makes 4 to 6 servings

NOTE

To roast garlic: Preheat the oven to 400°F (200°C). Cut off the top of the garlic head, exposing the cloves. Drizzle the top with a little olive oil and a sprinkle of salt. Loosely wrap the garlic in aluminum foil and roast for 45 minutes, or until fragrant and the bulb appears soft and golden. Remove from the oven and let cool. When cool enough to handle, squeeze the base of each clove to push out the roasted garlic.

BILL'S ARTICHOKE MAC AND CHIPS

Sauce

2½ to 3 cups (600 to 720 ml)
    unsweetened almond milk
1 to 1½ cups (140 to 210 g) unsalted raw
    cashews, soaked in hot water for
    30 minutes, well drained
¾ to 1 cup (173 to 230 g) vegan
    cream cheese
½ cup (30 g) nutritional yeast
2 tablespoons (34 g) white miso paste
2 tablespoons (23 g) roasted red
    bell pepper, or 1 tablespoon (16 g)
    tomato paste
2 tablespoons (30 ml) fresh
    lemon juice
2 teaspoons Dijon mustard
1½ teaspoons salt, plus more
    as needed
1 teaspoon onion powder
1 teaspoon garlic powder
1 teaspoon smoked paprika
¼ teaspoon ground turmeric

Olive oil or cooking oil spray, for
    preparing the baking dish

Pasta and Artichokes

16 ounces (454 g) cellentani, cavatappi,
    or other corkscrew pasta
2 to 3 (12-ounce, or 340 g) jars
    marinated artichoke hearts, drained,
    quartered, or coarsely chopped
1 tablespoon (9 g) capers
1 cup (56 g) crumbled potato chips

Our friend Bill loves artichokes, mac uncheese, and our local Route 11 potato chips. I came up with this recipe for his birthday dinner one year that combines all three of his favorites.

1. **To make the sauce:** In a high-speed blender, combine all the sauce ingredients. Purée until completely smooth. Taste and add more salt, as needed. Set aside.

2. Preheat the oven to 375°F (190°C). Lightly coat a 9 × 13-inch (23 × 33 cm) baking dish with olive oil or cooking oil spray. Set aside.

3. **To make the pasta and artichokes:** Bring a large pot of salted water to a boil over high heat. Add the pasta and cook according to the package directions until tender. Drain well and return it to the pot.

4. Add the artichokes, capers, and sauce to the pasta and gently stir to combine. Transfer the mac and cheese to the prepared baking dish.

5. Sprinkle the potato chips over the top, cover the baking dish with aluminum foil, and bake for 15 minutes, or until hot.

Makes 4 to 6 servings

CHAPTER 4

Meaty Macs

All the recipes in this book are hearty and satisfying, but the ones in this chapter are the heartiest of the bunch. Some, such as the Crabby Mac Uncheese (page 99) or the Mac and Stroganoff (page 116), are ideal company fare, while others, such as the Philly Cheesesteak Mac (page 102) and the Kid's Stuff Mac 'n' Cheese (page 105), made with vegan hot dogs and topped with crushed potato chips, are perfect weeknight meals for kids of all ages.

CHILI MAC

Chili

3 cups (594 g) cooked lentils or (516 g) black beans, or 2 (15.5-ounce, or 425 g) cans, rinsed and drained

1½ cups (390 g) tomato salsa (hot or mild)

3 tablespoons (48 g) Barbecue Sauce (page 101), or store-bought

2 to 3 teaspoons (5 to 8 g) chili powder, plus more as needed

Salt, to taste

Ground black pepper, to taste

Sauce

3 cups (720 ml) plain unsweetened nondairy milk

1¼ cups (175 g) unsalted raw cashews, soaked in boiling water for 30 minutes and drained

⅓ cup (20 g) nutritional yeast

2 tablespoons (30 ml) fresh lemon juice

1 teaspoon salt

½ teaspoon smoked paprika

½ teaspoon onion powder

½ teaspoon garlic powder

½ teaspoon chili powder

¼ teaspoon ground turmeric

Pasta

16 ounces (454 g) elbow macaroni, or other small pasta

Nonstick cooking spray, for preparing the baking dish

Toppings (optional)

¾ cup (47 g) crushed tortilla chips, or corn chips

1 ripe Haas avocado, peeled, pitted, and diced

This is a great way to use up leftover chili. If you don't have any on hand, this recipe includes a quick chili that can be ready in minutes.

1. **To make the chili:** In a saucepan over medium heat, combine all the chili ingredients. Cover the pan and cook, stirring occasionally, until heated through and the flavors are well blended, about 5 minutes. Add as much water as needed to create a sauce-like consistency and prevent the chili from sticking to the bottom of the pan. Reduce the heat to low and simmer, stirring frequently, until heated through and any raw taste from the chili powder is cooked off, about 15 minutes.

(continued)

(continued)

2. **To make the sauce:** In a high-speed blender, combine all the sauce ingredients. Blend until very smooth and creamy. Set aside.

3. **To make the pasta:** Bring a large pot of salted water to a boil over high heat. Add the pasta and cook according to the package directions until al dente. Drain the pasta and return to the pot.

4. Pour the sauce over the pasta and toss to combine.

5. Preheat the oven to 350°F (180°C). Lightly coat a 9 × 13-inch (23 × 33 cm) baking dish with cooking spray.

6. Spread the pasta mixture into the prepared baking dish. Spread the chili evenly on top of the pasta.

7. **To finish:** Sprinkle the tortilla chips on top of the chili. Bake for 20 minutes until hot. Serve topped with the avocado.

Makes 4 to 6 servings

VARIATION

Mac & Cheeseburger

For a change of pace, omit the chili and add 8 ounces (225 g) vegan burger crumbles and 2 cups (168 g) shredded vegan cheddar to the cooked macaroni. Stir in the sauce, heat through, and you've got a Mac & Cheeseburger!

CRABBY MAC UNCHEESE

Nonstick cooking spray

16 ounces (454 g) rotini, or other small pasta

2 tablespoons (28 g) vegan butter

1½ cups (105 g) sliced fresh mushrooms

½ cup (80 g) minced onion

½ of a green bell pepper, minced

¼ cup (30 g) minced celery

Salt, to taste

Ground black pepper, to taste

2 tablespoons (16 g) all-purpose flour

3 cups (720 ml) plain unsweetened nondairy milk

1 (14-ounce, or 395 g) jar hearts of palm, well drained, patted dry, and roughly chopped

1 (6-ounce, or 170 g) jar marinated artichoke hearts, well drained, patted dry, and roughly chopped

⅓ cup (80 g) vegan mayonnaise

2 tablespoons (8 g) chopped fresh parsley, plus more for garnish

2 teaspoons Old Bay seasoning

1½ teaspoons nori, or dulse, flakes

1 teaspoon prepared yellow mustard

½ cup (27 g) oyster crackers, well crushed

Paprika, for garnish

I make my favorite plant-based crab cakes with hearts of palm and artichokes, and I've discovered they also make a great addition to mac uncheese. Old Bay seasoning and nori or dulse flakes provide a subtle taste of the sea.

1. Coat a 9 × 13-inch (23 × 33 cm) baking dish with cooking spray. Set aside.

2. Bring a large pot of salted water to a boil over high heat. Add the pasta and cook according to the package directions until al dente. Drain well and return to the pot.

3. Preheat the oven to 350°F (180°C).

4. In a large skillet over medium heat, melt the butter.

5. Add the mushrooms, onion, bell pepper, and celery and season with salt and pepper. Cook, stirring frequently, until tender, about 7 minutes. Stir in the flour.

6. Slowly add the milk, stirring to combine, and bring to a boil. Reduce the heat to maintain a simmer and cook, stirring, for 2 minutes, or until thickened. Remove from the heat.

7. Stir in the hearts of palm, artichoke hearts, mayo, parsley, Old Bay seasoning, nori flakes, and mustard and season with salt and pepper. Mix well and add to the cooked pasta. Toss to coat. Transfer the mixture to the prepared baking dish. Bake for 20 minutes, or until bubbly.

8. Sprinkle with the crushed crackers, paprika, and parsley when ready to serve.

Makes 4 to 6 servings

BBQ JACK AND MAC

Jackfruit BBQ

1 tablespoon (15 ml) olive oil

1 yellow onion, minced

1 (16-ounce, or 454 g) can water-packed jackfruit, drained and shredded, or thinly sliced

1 tablespoon (15 ml) tamari

¼ teaspoon smoked paprika

Salt and ground black pepper, to taste

1½ to 2 cups (375 to 500 g) Barbecue Sauce (page 101), or store-bought

Sauce

3 cups (720 ml) plain unsweetened nondairy milk

1¼ cups (175 g) unsalted raw cashews, soaked in boiling water for 30 minutes and drained

⅓ cup (20 g) nutritional yeast

2 tablespoons (30 ml) fresh lemon juice

1 teaspoon salt

½ teaspoon smoked paprika

½ teaspoon onion powder

½ teaspoon garlic powder

½ teaspoon chili powder

¼ teaspoon ground turmeric

Pasta

16 ounces (454 g) penne, or other small pasta

Topping

1 cup (56 g) crushed vegan barbecue potato chips

Jackfruit makes the best barbecue thanks to its meaty texture and ability to absorb flavors. The tangy Barbecue Sauce (opposite) is the perfect foil to the creamy mac uncheese.

1. **To make the jackfruit BBQ:** In a large skillet over medium heat, heat the olive oil.

2. Add the onion and cook until softened, about 5 minutes.

3. Add the jackfruit and cook until softened, about 5 minutes. Stir in the tamari and paprika and season with salt and pepper.

4. Add about 1½ cups (375 g) of barbecue sauce, stirring well to mix. Use a fork (or two) to break up the jackfruit more, as needed. Cook for about 5 minutes, stirring occasionally, to heat through and blend the flavors.

5. **To make the sauce:** In a high-speed blender, combine all the sauce ingredients and blend until very smooth and creamy. Set aside.

6. **To make the pasta:** Bring a large pot of salted water to a boil over high heat. Add the pasta and cook according to the package directions until al dente. Drain well and return to the pot. Pour the sauce over the pasta and toss to combine. Place the pot over low heat and cook for about 3 minutes, stirring, to heat through and thicken the sauce slightly.

7. Spoon the jackfruit into the bottom of a large serving dish. Top with the pasta mixture, spreading it evenly.

8. **To finish:** Sprinkle the top with the barbecue potato chips and serve.

Makes 4 to 6 servings

BARBECUE SAUCE

1 tablespoon (15 ml) olive oil

1 small yellow onion, minced

2 garlic cloves, minced

1 (14.5-ounce, or 410 g) can tomato sauce or purée

1 tablespoon (17 g) chipotle chile in adobo sauce, finely minced

2 tablespoons (40 g) pure maple syrup, or (30 g) dark brown sugar, plus more as needed

2 tablespoons (30 ml) tamari

2 tablespoons (30 ml) apple cider vinegar, plus more as needed

2 tablespoons (30 ml) water

Salt, to taste

Ground black pepper, to taste

¼ teaspoon liquid smoke

This is my favorite homemade barbecue sauce—not too sweet, not too spicy. Feel free to make it hotter or sweeter to suit your own taste.

1. In a saucepan over medium heat, heat the olive oil.

2. Add the onion and garlic and cook for 5 minutes, until the vegetables soften.

3. Add the tomato sauce, chipotle, maple syrup, tamari, vinegar, and water and season with salt and pepper. Stir well to combine. Simmer for 15 minutes, or until the sauce reduces to the desired consistency. Near the end of the cooking time, stir in the liquid smoke, taste, and adjust the seasoning, adding more salt, maple syrup, or vinegar, as needed, to balance the flavors.

Makes about 2 cups (500 g)

PHILLY CHEESESTEAK MAC

1 tablespoon (15 ml) olive oil

1 small yellow onion, thinly sliced

6 portobello mushroom caps,
    thinly sliced

1 small red bell pepper, cored, seeded,
    and thinly sliced

¼ cup (60 g) ketchup

1 tablespoon (15 ml) vegan
    Worcestershire sauce, or tamari

Salt, to taste

Ground black pepper, to taste

16 ounces (454 g) penne, or other
    small pasta

1 recipe Cheddary Sauce (page 103),
    warm

If you're a fan of hearty mac uncheese, this one's for you with all the great flavors of a Philly cheesesteak. Thinly sliced and sautéed portobello mushrooms are the "steak" of choice, but substitute thinly sliced seitan if you prefer.

1. In a large skillet over medium-high heat, heat the olive oil.

2. Add the onion and cook until softened, about 5 minutes.

3. Add the mushrooms and red bell pepper and cook, stirring occasionally, until softened, about 5 minutes.

4. Stir in the ketchup and Worcestershire sauce and season with salt and pepper. Cook for 5 minutes more, or until the vegetables are very soft. Keep warm.

5. Bring a large pot of salted water to a boil over high heat. Add the pasta and cook according to the package directions until al dente. Drain well and return to the pot.

6. Add about half of the Cheddary Sauce to the pasta and toss to combine. Transfer the pasta to a 3½-quart (3.3 L) serving dish. Spoon the mushroom mixture evenly over the pasta. Drizzle with the remaining sauce and serve hot.

Makes 4 to 6 servings

CHEDDARY SAUCE

1 cup (140 g) unsalted raw cashews

1 large russet potato, peeled and diced

1 small carrot, chopped

½ of a small yellow onion, chopped

1 garlic clove, chopped

1 teaspoon salt

⅓ cup (20 g) nutritional yeast, plus more as needed

2 tablespoons (28 g) vegan butter

1 tablespoon (15 ml) rice vinegar

1 tablespoon (15 ml) fresh lemon juice

1½ teaspoons white miso paste

½ teaspoon prepared yellow mustard

½ teaspoon onion powder

½ teaspoon smoked paprika

¼ teaspoon ground turmeric

1 cup (240 ml) plain unsweetened nondairy milk, or water

Use this flavorful sauce to make the Philly Cheesesteak Mac (opposite) or as the base for virtually any mac uncheese you like. The sauce is also great drizzled over your favorite roasted vegetables, baked potatoes, or nachos.

1. In a saucepan, combine the cashews, potato, carrot, onion, garlic, and salt with enough water to cover. Place the pan over high heat and bring to a boil. Reduce the heat to maintain a simmer and cook until the vegetables are soft, 10 to 15 minutes.

2. Using a slotted spoon, transfer the cooked vegetables and cashews to a high-speed blender, reserving the cooking water.

3. Add the remaining ingredients and blend until smooth and creamy, stopping to scrape down the sides, as needed. Add as much of the reserved cooking water as needed to achieve the consistency you prefer for the sauce. Taste and adjust the seasoning, as needed. The sauce is now ready to use.

Makes about 4 cups (900 g)

1 + 1 = YUM

1 recipe Cheddary Sauce + 1 box small pasta, cooked = 1 delicious vegan mac & cheese dinner for 4 or 6

KID'S STUFF MAC 'N' CHEESE

Pasta

16 ounces (454 g) elbow macaroni, or
   other small pasta

Sauce

3 cups (720 ml) water, or
   vegetable broth
1 large russet potato, peeled and diced
1 small carrot, chopped
¾ cup (105 g) unsalted raw cashews
½ of a small yellow onion, chopped
½ teaspoon salt
¼ cup (15 g) nutritional yeast
2 tablespoons (28 g) vegan butter
1 tablespoon (15 ml) fresh lemon juice
½ teaspoon prepared yellow mustard
¼ teaspoon ground turmeric
¼ teaspoon smoked paprika
¼ teaspoon ground black pepper
2 vegan hot dogs, cooked and cut into
   ¼-inch (6 mm) slices

Topping

2 cups (112 g) crushed potato chips

Children of all ages will love this mac uncheese featuring sliced hot dogs and a crushed potato chip topping.

1. **To make the pasta:** Bring a large pot of salted water to a boil over high heat. Add the pasta and cook according to the package directions until al dente. Drain well and set aside.

2. **To make the sauce:** In the same pot over high heat, combine the water, potato, carrot, cashews, onion, and salt and bring to a boil. Reduce the heat to maintain a simmer and cook until the vegetables are soft, 10 to 15 minutes. Carefully transfer the contents of the pot to a high-speed blender.

3. Add the nutritional yeast, butter, lemon juice, mustard, turmeric, paprika, and pepper. Blend until completely smooth, stopping to scrape down the sides, as needed.

4. Return the pasta to the pot. Add the hot dog slices and pour the sauce on top. Gently stir to combine and coat the pasta and hot dogs with the sauce. Place the pot over low heat and cook until hot.

5. **To finish:** Sprinkle the top with the crushed potato chips and serve.

Makes 4 to 6 servings

BAKED VARIATION

Preheat the oven to 350°F (180°C). Coat a 3½- to 4-quart (3.3 to 3.8 L) baking dish with nonstick cooking oil spray. Transfer the mac uncheese to the prepared baking dish and sprinkle the potato chips on top. Bake until hot and golden on top, about 20 minutes. Serve immediately.

SHEPHERD'S MAC

Lentils
1 tablespoon (15 ml) olive oil
2½ cups (175 g) chopped mushrooms
2½ cups (495 g) cooked lentils
2½ cups (338 g) frozen mixed
  vegetables, steamed
2 tablespoons (30 ml) tamari, divided
½ teaspoon onion powder
½ teaspoon garlic powder
Salt and ground black pepper, to taste

Pasta
16 ounces (454 g) radiatore, or other
  small pasta

Sauce
2½ cups (600 ml) water
1 large russet potato, peeled and diced
1 small carrot, chopped
¾ cup (105 g) unsalted raw cashews
½ of a small yellow onion, chopped
2 garlic cloves, smashed
Salt, to taste
½ cup (30 g) nutritional yeast
2 tablespoons (28 g) vegan butter
1 tablespoon (15 ml) fresh lemon juice
½ teaspoon prepared yellow mustard
¼ teaspoon ground turmeric
¼ teaspoon smoked paprika
Ground black pepper, to taste

Topping
Toasted Panko Crumbs (page 25)

If you enjoy both shepherd's pie and mac uncheese, chances are you'll love this nontraditional union of the two in one delicious casserole.

1. Preheat the oven to 375°F (190°C).

2. **To make the lentils:** In a skillet over medium heat, heat the olive oil. Add the mushrooms and cook until soft, about 4 minutes. Stir in the lentils, mixed vegetables, 1 tablespoon (15 ml) of the tamari, the onion powder, and garlic powder and season with salt and pepper. Stir well to mix. Cook, stirring, for 2 minutes to blend the flavors. Remove from the heat and set aside.

3. **To make the pasta:** Bring a large pot of salted water to a boil over high heat. Add the pasta and cook according to the package directions until al dente. Drain well and set aside.

4. **To make the sauce:** In the same pot over high heat, combine the water, potato, carrot, cashews, onion, and garlic and season with salt. Bring to a boil. Reduce the heat to maintain a simmer, cover the pot, and cook until the vegetables are soft, 10 to 15 minutes. Carefully transfer the contents of the pot to a high-speed blender.

5. Add the nutritional yeast, butter, lemon juice, remaining 1 tablespoon (15 ml) of tamari, mustard, turmeric, and paprika and season with the pepper. Blend until completely smooth, stopping to scrape down the sides, as needed.

6. Return the pasta to the pot. Pour the sauce over the pasta and gently stir to combine.

7. Transfer the lentil mixture to a 9 × 13-inch (23 × 33 cm) baking dish, spreading it evenly. Spread the pasta mixture on top.

8. **To finish:** Sprinkle the top with the Toasted Panko Crumbs. Bake for 20 minutes. Serve hot.

Makes 4 to 6 servings

LOBSTER MUSHROOM MAC UNCHEESE

16 ounces (454 g) cavatappi, or other small pasta

2 cups (150 g) lobster mushrooms, fresh or reconstituted from dried, trimmed

1 tablespoon (15 ml) olive oil

Salt, to taste

Ground black pepper, to taste

1 yellow onion, minced

1 celery stalk, minced

2 garlic cloves, minced

1¾ cups (420 ml) vegetable broth, plus more as needed

2 teaspoons tomato paste

¼ cup (60 ml) brandy, or dry white wine

1 cup (240 g) Cashew Cream (page 109)

½ cup (120 ml) plain unsweetened nondairy milk

1 tablespoon (3 g) minced fresh chives

Although fresh lobster mushrooms can be difficult to find (try Whole Foods), dried ones can be easier to locate at specialty food stores or online. Regular white mushrooms or oyster mushrooms may be substituted for up to half the lobster mushrooms.

1. Bring a large pot of salted water to a boil over high heat. Add the pasta and cook according to the package directions until al dente. Drain well and return to the pot.

2. Cut the reddish part of the lobster mushrooms into bite-size pieces until you have 1 cup (75 g). Set aside. Finely chop the remaining mushrooms and set aside.

3. In a large saucepan over medium heat, heat the olive oil.

4. Add the reddish bite-size mushroom pieces and cook, stirring, for 3 to 4 minutes. Season with salt and pepper, and add to the reserved pasta. Return the saucepan to the heat. Add the onion, celery, and garlic, and cook until softened, about 5 minutes, adding a little vegetable broth if the vegetables begin to stick. Add the remaining finely chopped mushrooms and cook for 2 minutes more.

5. Stir in the tomato paste until well combined and cook, stirring, for 2 minutes. Remove from the heat and stir in the brandy. Add the vegetable broth and season with salt and pepper. Place the pan over high heat and bring to a boil. Reduce the heat to low, cover the pan, and simmer for 15 minutes. Carefully transfer the mushroom mixture to a blender or food processor and blend until smooth.

6. Add the cashew cream and milk and blend to combine. Pour the sauce over the pasta and stir to coat. Place the pot over medium heat and cook, stirring, until hot. Transfer to a 3½- to 4-quart (3.3 to 3.8 L) serving dish and sprinkle with the chives. Serve hot.

Makes 4 to 6 servings

CASHEW CREAM

1 cup (140 g) raw cashew pieces, soaked in boiling hot water for 30 minutes and drained
½ cup (120 ml) water, plus more as needed

Blending soaked and drained raw cashews with water creates a sublime creamy sauce that can be used in all sorts of recipes, including your favorite mac uncheese, to which it adds a decadent richness.

In a high-speed blender, combine the drained cashews and water. Blend until smooth and creamy. The cashew cream should be very thick. For a thinner cream, add a little more water, 1 tablespoon (15 ml) at a time, to reach your desired consistency.

Makes about 1½ cups (360 g)

VEGAN SOUR CREAM

¾ cup (105 g) unsalted raw cashews, soaked in hot water for 30 minutes and drained
⅓ cup (80 ml) plain unsweetened nondairy milk
2 tablespoons (30 ml) apple cider vinegar
1½ tablespoons (21 g) refined coconut oil, melted
¼ teaspoon salt

This cashew-based sour cream works well in the Mac and Stroganoff (page 116) or as an extra topping for Chili Mac (page 96).

In a high-speed blender, combine all the ingredients and blend until very smooth. Transfer the mixture to a container, tightly cover, and refrigerate for at least 2 hours to chill and thicken before use. Keep refrigerated for up to 5 days.

Makes about 1 cup (230 g)

BRAT & KRAUT MAC & CHEESE

Pasta

16 ounces (454 g) elbow macaroni, or other small pasta

Sauce

2 tablespoons (30 ml) olive oil, divided, plus more for the baking dish

1 cup (140 g) unsalted raw cashews, soaked in boiling water for 30 minutes and drained

1½ cups (360 ml) plain unsweetened nondairy milk

1¼ cups (300 ml) vegetable broth

3 tablespoons (11 g) nutritional yeast

1 tablespoon (15 ml) fresh lemon juice

½ teaspoon ground turmeric

Salt, to taste

Ground black pepper, to taste

1 small onion, chopped

3 garlic cloves, minced

2 cups (284 g) sauerkraut, well drained

2 Vegan Bratwurst (page 112) or store-bought, sliced

Smoked paprika, for garnish

This is one of the heartiest recipes in the book, and a good choice for cold weather fare. I prefer to make my own bratwurst (see Vegan Bratwurst, page 112), but there are many good brands available, if you prefer to buy them. If you're not a fan of plant-based sausage, just leave it out—you can still make this delicious casserole without the brats.

1. **To make the pasta:** Bring a large pot of salted water to a boil over high heat. Add the pasta and cook according to the package directions until al dente. Drain well and return to the pot.

2. **To make the sauce:** Preheat the oven to 350°F (180°C). Lightly coat a 9 × 13-inch (23 × 33 cm) baking dish with olive oil. Set aside.

3. In a high-speed blender, combine the cashews, milk, vegetable broth, nutritional yeast, lemon juice, and turmeric and season with salt and pepper. Blend until smooth, stopping to scrape down the sides, as needed. Set aside.

4. In a large skillet over medium heat, heat 1 tablespoon (15 ml) of the olive oil.

5. Add the onion and garlic and cook until soft, about 5 minutes. Stir in the sauerkraut and transfer the mixture to the blender along with the cashew mixture. Blend until smooth.

6. Return the skillet to medium heat, and heat the remaining 1 tablespoon (15 ml) of olive oil.

7. Add the bratwurst slices and cook until brown on both sides, turning once. Add the bratwurst and the sauce to the reserved pasta, stirring well to coat with the sauce. Taste and adjust the seasoning, as needed. Transfer to the prepared baking dish, spreading it evenly. Sprinkle with smoked paprika, cover the baking dish with aluminum foil, and bake for 20 minutes. Serve hot.

Makes 4 to 6 servings

VEGAN BRATWURST

⅓ cup (52 g) old-fashioned rolled oats

1 cup (120 g) vital wheat gluten, plus more as needed

¼ cup (15 g) nutritional yeast

1 tablespoon (7 g) ground flaxseed

1 teaspoon onion powder

½ teaspoon salt

½ teaspoon caraway seed

½ teaspoon celery seed

½ teaspoon ground coriander

½ teaspoon ground fennel seed

½ teaspoon dried oregano, or rubbed sage

½ teaspoon garlic powder

½ teaspoon smoked paprika

¼ teaspoon ground nutmeg, or allspice

¼ teaspoon ground black pepper

1 cup (256 g) cooked or canned cannellini beans, well drained

1 tablespoon (17 g) white miso paste

1 tablespoon (15 ml) tamari

¾ cup (180 ml) water, plain unsweetened nondairy milk, or beer, plus more as needed

There are a number of vegan bratwurst brands currently available in well-stocked supermarkets. However, if you prefer to make your own, here's an easy recipe.

1. Pulse the oats in a food processor until coarsely chopped. Add the wheat gluten, nutritional yeast, flaxseed, onion powder, salt, caraway seed, celery seed, coriander, fennel seed, oregano, garlic powder, paprika, nutmeg, and pepper. Pulse to mix well.

2. Add the cannellini beans, miso, tamari, and water and pulse until evenly moistened. If the mixture seems too dry, add a little more water; if it seems too wet, add a little more vital wheat gluten. Transfer the mixture to a work surface and knead for 1 to 2 minutes.

3. Place a steamer basket in a large pot. Add enough water to bring it just below the steamer basket. Place the pot over high heat and bring to a simmer. Place a square sheet of aluminum foil on the counter, and place about ½ cup (115 g) of the bratwurst mixture onto it. Shape into a tube, fold the bottom edge of the foil over the brat, and roll it up. Roll the tube back and forth, pressing lightly with your hands, to give it an even shape, and then twist the ends closed. Repeat with the remaining mixture to form six brats, wrapping each individually with aluminum foil and twisting the ends. Arrange the bratwursts in the top of the steamer basket (it's okay to stack them). Cover the pot, reduce the heat to maintain a simmer, and steam for 45 minutes.

4. Remove the bratwursts from the heat and transfer to a plate. Discard the foil and let them cool to room temperature. If not using right away, cover and refrigerate until needed, up to 5 days—they will become firmer in the refrigerator. You can also lightly pan-fry the brats to make them firmer and nicely browned.

Makes 6 brats

JERK TEMPEH MAC

16 ounces (454 g) elbow macaroni, or other small pasta
Nonstick cooking spray
1 teaspoon salt
1 teaspoon chili powder
½ teaspoon dried thyme
½ teaspoon garlic powder
¼ teaspoon ground black pepper
¼ teaspoon ground allspice
¼ teaspoon ground cinnamon
¼ teaspoon ground nutmeg
¼ teaspoon ground ginger
2 tablespoons (30 ml) olive oil
8 ounces (225 g) tempeh, steamed for 10 minutes and diced
1 jalapeño pepper, seeded and minced
1 scallion, white and green parts, chopped
1 tablespoon (20 g) blackstrap molasses
1 tablespoon (15 ml) fresh lime juice
4 tablespoons (56 g) vegan butter
¼ cup (31 g) all-purpose flour
3 cups (720 ml) plain unsweetened nondairy milk
1 cup (240 ml) vegetable broth
¼ cup (15 g) nutritional yeast

This zesty mac uncheese is like treating your taste buds to an exotic vacation. Meaty tempeh seasoned with heady jerk spices is the star of this show. If you're not a fan of heat, leave out the jalapeño; for more heat, use a habanero instead.

1. Bring a large pot of salted water to a boil over high heat. Add the pasta and cook according to the package directions until al dente. Drain well and set aside.

2. Preheat the oven to 350°F (180°C). Lightly coat a 3½- to 4-quart (3.3 to 3.8 L) baking dish with cooking spray. Set aside.

3. In a small bowl, stir together the salt, chili powder, thyme, garlic powder, pepper, allspice, cinnamon, nutmeg, and ginger. Set aside.

4. In a skillet over medium heat, heat the olive oil.

5. Add the tempeh and cook until browned, about 5 minutes.

6. Stir in the jalapeño and scallion and cook for 2 minutes. Add the spice mix and stir to coat. Stir in the molasses and lime juice. Remove from the heat and set aside.

7. Return the pasta pot to medium heat and add the butter to melt. Whisk in the flour and cook, whisking constantly, for 2 minutes.

8. Slowly add the milk and vegetable broth, whisking until incorporated. Reduce the heat to low and continue to cook, whisking, until the sauce begins to thicken, about 5 minutes. Remove from the heat and add the tempeh mixture and nutritional yeast. Stir to combine. Taste and adjust the seasoning, as needed.

9. Add the cooked pasta to the pot and stir to combine. Transfer the mixture to the prepared baking dish. Bake for 20 minutes, or until hot.

Makes 4 to 6 servings

TETRAZZINI MAC

16 ounces (454 g) fettucine noodles, broken in half

Nonstick cooking spray

½ cup (70 g) unsalted raw cashews, soaked in boiling water for 30 minutes and drained

½ cup (120 ml) hot water

8 ounces (225 g) silken tofu

¼ cup (60 ml) dry sherry, or white wine

2 tablespoons (7.5 g) nutritional yeast

Salt, to taste

1 tablespoon (15 ml) olive oil

2 garlic cloves, chopped

8 ounces (225 g) sliced mushrooms

Ground black pepper, to taste

½ cup (65 g) frozen peas

4 tablespoons (56 g) vegan butter

¼ cup (31 g) all-purpose flour

2 cups (480 ml) vegetable broth

2 cups (720 ml) plain unsweetened nondairy milk

½ cup (72.5 g) roasted almonds, ground or chopped

2 tablespoons (8 g) fresh parsley

A touch of sherry and ground roasted almonds elevate this creamy noodle casserole to company fare. Serve with a crisp green salad for a delicious meal.

1. Bring a large pot of salted water to a boil over high heat. Add the pasta and cook according to the package directions until al dente. Drain well and return to the pot. Set aside.

2. Preheat the oven to 350°F (180°C). Coat a 9 × 13-inch (23 × 33 cm) glass baking dish with cooking spray. Set aside.

3. In a high-speed blender, combine the cashews and hot water and blend until smooth. Add the tofu, sherry, and nutritional yeast and season with salt. Blend until smooth. Set aside.

4. In a saucepan over medium-high heat, heat the olive oil.

5. Add the garlic, then stir in the mushrooms. Cook until the mushrooms release their liquid and it evaporates, about 5 minutes. Season with salt and pepper. Add the mushrooms to the pasta, stir in the peas, and set aside.

6. Return the saucepan to low heat and add the butter to melt. Cook for 1 minute, stirring, and then whisk in the flour and cook for 1 minute more. Slowly whisk in the vegetable broth and milk. Bring to a boil and season with salt and pepper.

7. Slowly whisk the cashew-tofu mixture into the sauce, whisking until there are no clumps. Taste and adjust the seasoning, as needed. Cook the sauce 2 minutes more to thicken a bit. Add the sauce to the pasta and vegetables, stirring to combine. Place the pot over low heat and cook for 2 to 3 minutes. Taste and adjust the seasoning, as needed. Spread the mixture into the prepared baking dish.

8. Sprinkle the top with the almonds. Bake for 20 minutes. Serve hot garnished with parsley.

Makes 4 to 6 servings

MAC AND STROGANOFF

2 tablespoons (30 ml) olive oil

1 large yellow onion, chopped

1 large green bell pepper, cored, seeded, and chopped

1 pound (454 g) white mushrooms, coarsely chopped

2 tablespoons (16 g) unbleached all-purpose flour

1 tablespoon (8 g) sweet Hungarian paprika

2 tablespoons (32 g) tomato paste

1 tablespoon (15 ml) tamari

2 cups (480 ml) vegetable broth, divided

1 cup (240 ml) plain unsweetened non-dairy milk

Salt, to taste

Ground black pepper, to taste

1 cup (230 g) Vegan Sour Cream (page 109) or store-bought, plus more for serving

2 tablespoons (8 g) minced fresh parsley

16 ounces (454 g) fettucine noodles, broken in half

Traditional stroganoff features a creamy sauce and is served over noodles, so it wasn't much of a stretch to come up with Mac and Stroganoff. If you can find egg-free egg noodles (yes, it's a thing), use them, but the recipe calls for readily available fettucine noodles.

1. In a large skillet over medium heat, heat the olive oil.

2. Add the onion and green bell pepper and cook until softened, about 5 minutes.

3. Add the mushrooms and cook until softened, about 3 minutes. Sprinkle on the flour and paprika and cook, stirring, for about 1 minute to remove the raw taste from the flour.

4. In a small bowl, stir together the tomato paste, tamari, and ½ cup (120 ml) of the vegetable broth, blending until smooth. Add the tomato paste mixture to the vegetables, stirring until smooth. Add the remaining 1½ cups (360 ml) of broth and bring to a boil. Reduce the heat to low, stir in the milk, and season with salt and pepper. Simmer, uncovered, until the flavors meld and the sauce begins to thicken, about 15 minutes.

5. While the stroganoff simmers, make the pasta: Bring a large pot of salted water to a boil over high heat. Add the pasta and cook according to the package directions until al dente. Drain well and return to the pot.

6. Slowly whisk the sour cream into the stroganoff until well blended. Add the stroganoff to the cooked pasta and toss to combine. Transfer to a large serving bowl and sprinkle with the parsley. Serve hot with more sour cream on the side.

Makes 4 to 6 servings

MAC AND SPEEDY

4 cups (960 ml) plain unsweetened
    plant milk
1 cup (240 ml) water
Salt, to taste
16 ounces (454 g) elbow macaroni
3 cups (approximately 335 g, weights
    will vary) of your favorite shredded
    vegan cheddar cheese

For the easiest, speediest, vegan mac and cheese, cook your macaroni in unsweetened plant milk and stir in vegan cheddar cheese shreds. Dinner is served.

1. In a large pot, bring the milk, water, and salt to a boil.

2. Add the macaroni, reduce the heat to a simmer, and stir constantly until the pasta is cooked, about 10 minutes.

3. Turn off the heat and then stir in the cheddar shreds until the cheese is melted and the macaroni is evenly coated.

Makes 4 to 6 servings

MAKE IT MEATY

To transform any basic vegan mac and cheese recipe into a meaty meal, sauté a package of vegan beefy crumbles (Gardein or Beyond Meat brands are good) and stir it into the cooked macaroni when adding the cheesy sauce. For added flavor, season the crumbles with taco seasoning and add chopped tomatoes for a tasty taco mac and cheese.

CHAPTER 5
Fun with Mac & Cheese

If there are fewer than four people in your family, chances are there will be leftovers when you make mac uncheese. At my house, that's never a problem— I usually just heat up the leftovers the next day and they disappear. If you want to have some fun with your leftovers, try the recipes in this chapter to transform your leftover mac uncheese into something completely different. If you don't have any leftovers on hand, whip up a batch of a favorite mac uncheese, such as the One-Pot Cheesy Mac (page 39), to use in these recipes.

This chapter also includes two creamy noodle-centric desserts, as well as a Cheesy Mac Mug (page 120) recipe to satisfy mac uncheese cravings in minutes.

CHEESY MAC MUG

½ cup (52.5 g) elbow macaroni
½ cup (120 ml) water
Salt, to taste
¼ cup (60 ml) plain unsweetened
    nondairy milk
Pinch dried mustard
⅓ cup (37 g) shredded vegan cheddar
    cheese, or Cheddary Sauce (page
    103, see note)
Ground black pepper, to taste

This recipe is for those times when you crave a little comfort food. It's ideal for a late-night snack or quick anytime meal. It's also a great way to make a small amount of mac uncheese to use in the other recipes in this chapter when you don't have any leftovers. This needs to be made in a large mug to avoid the water boiling over in the microwave—if you don't have a large mug, use a bowl.

1. In a large microwavable mug or bowl, combine the pasta, water, and a pinch of salt. Microwave on high power for 2 minutes and then stir. Continue microwaving in 2-minute intervals, stirring between each, until the pasta is tender. If the pasta absorbs all the water before it is cooked, add another 2 tablespoons (30 ml) of water. The water should be absorbed completely and the pasta cooked through.

2. Carefully remove the hot mug or bowl from the microwave and stir in the milk, mustard, and Cheddary Sauce. Season with salt and pepper. Microwave for 1 minute more to melt the cheese. Stir to mix well. Serve hot.

Makes 1 serving

NOTE
If you don't want to use shredded vegan cheese, replace it with ½ cup (115 g) of Cheddary Sauce (page 103) and reduce the milk by half.

MAC UNCHEESE OMELET

¾ cup (90 g) chickpea flour
¼ teaspoon baking powder
¼ teaspoon garlic powder
Salt, to taste
Ground black pepper, to taste
¾ cup (180 ml) water
1 tablespoon (15 ml) olive oil
1 plum tomato, chopped
2 scallions, white and green parts, minced
1 cup (30 g) packed chopped baby spinach
½ to ¾ cup (weight varies) leftover or homemade mac uncheese, warmed
¼ cup (57 g) Cheddary Sauce (page 103), warmed
2 tablespoons (8 g) chopped fresh parsley, or (5 g) basil

Just a small amount of leftover mac uncheese goes a long way as a unique filling in this delicious omelet made with chickpea flour. If you don't have any leftover mac uncheese, make the quick Cheesy Mac Mug (page 120) to use in this recipe.

1. In a large bowl, combine the chickpea flour, baking powder, and garlic powder and season with salt and pepper. Mix well. Add the water and stir until no clumps remain. Set aside.

2. In a nonstick skillet over medium-high heat, heat the olive oil.

3. Add the tomato, scallions, and spinach and cook, stirring, for 1 minute to wilt the spinach.

4. Pour the batter into the skillet and spread it out into a thin circle. Cook for 3 minutes, carefully flip (see Note), and cook for 3 more minutes.

5. Spread the mac uncheese evenly on one side of the omelet. Fold the other side over the pasta and transfer the omelet to a plate.

6. Drizzle the Cheddary Sauce on top and sprinkle with the parsley. Serve hot.

Makes 1 omelet

NOTE

If you have trouble flipping the omelet, place a dinner plate over the omelet in the skillet and invert it. You can then transfer the omelet back into the skillet to cook the other side.

WAFFLED MAC UNCHEESE

Nonstick cooking oil spray
4 cups (weight varies) leftover or
   homemade mac uncheese, warmed
Hot sauce, for serving

These waffles make a hearty brunch or supper doused with hot sauce. Or try them topped with fried vegan seitan strips and brown gravy for a taste of the South. This recipe is a great way to use up leftover mac uncheese. No leftovers? Whip up a batch of One-Pot Cheesy Mac (page 39) to use.

1. Coat a rimmed baking sheet with nonstick cooking spray.

2. Spread the warm mac uncheese onto the prepared sheet and flatten it with a spatula. Refrigerate until completely set, about 30 minutes.

3. Preheat a waffle iron according to the manufacturer's instructions.

4. Carefully cut the mac uncheese into eight equal squares. Using a wide spatula, carefully lift one square and place it in the waffle iron. Top with a second square. Close the iron and cook until golden brown on both sides, about 5 minutes. Carefully remove the waffle and keep warm. Repeat with the remaining waffles. Serve hot with hot sauce.

Makes 4 servings

CHEESY BROCCOLI MAC SOUP

1 tablespoon (15 ml) olive oil

1 small yellow onion, minced

2 garlic cloves, minced

4 cups (960 ml) vegetable broth

3 cups (weight varies) leftover or homemade mac uncheese

1½ cups (340 g) Cheddary Sauce (page 103)

½ cup (120 ml) plain unsweetened nondairy milk

¼ teaspoon smoked paprika

Salt, to taste

Ground black pepper, to taste

2 cups (160 g) steamed small broccoli florets

¼ cup (32 g) Nut Parm (page 55)

Cheesy broccoli soup is a cold weather favorite in our house, so it was a no-brainer to try it made with leftover mac uncheese. The results were so good, this is now our go-to way to make it. We especially like that the broth isn't too thick (which it often is in cheesy soups). If you prefer a thicker broth, simply use less vegetable broth. To make this recipe without leftovers, I suggest using the quick and easy recipe for One-Pot Cheesy Mac (page 39).

1. In a large saucepan over medium heat, heat the olive oil.

2. Add the onion and cook until softened, about 5 minutes. Stir in the garlic and cook until fragrant, about 30 seconds.

3. Add the vegetable broth and bring to a boil. Reduce the heat to low, cover the pan, and simmer for 15 minutes.

4. Stir in the mac uncheese and then add the Cheddary Sauce, stirring until thoroughly combined.

5. Add the milk and paprika and season with salt and pepper. Cook, stirring, until hot.

6. Stir in the broccoli and serve hot, sprinkled with the Nut Parm.

Makes 4 to 6 servings

NOTE

The Cheddary Sauce (page 103) freezes really well, so make an extra batch to keep on hand for this soup. After thawing, it stirs up nice and creamy.

MAC UNCHEESE BALLS

2 tablespoons (28 g) vegan butter
½ cup (62 g) plus 2 tablespoons (16 g) all-purpose flour, divided
¾ cup (180 ml) plain unsweetened nondairy milk
1 packed cup (weight varies) leftover or homemade mac uncheese (see headnote)
Salt, to taste
Neutral vegetable oil, for frying
2 tablespoons (14 g) ground flaxseed
⅓ cup (80 ml) hot water
1 cup (50 g) panko bread crumbs

This recipe works best with a mac uncheese made with elbow macaroni or other small pasta shape. If you don't have any leftovers, the recipe for Cheesy Mac Mug (page 120) makes enough to use here.

1. In a small saucepan over medium-low heat, melt the butter. Add 2 tablespoons (16 g) of flour and stir until well mixed and bubbling.

2. Slowly whisk in the milk until it's fully blended with no lumps. Use a silicone spatula to continuously scrape the bottom of the pan to keep the sauce from burning. When thick and bubbly, remove from the heat and stir in the mac uncheese. Taste and add salt, as needed. Let cool to room temperature and then refrigerate for at least 3 hours to firm up.

3. Use a spoon to scoop out a 1½-inch (3.5 cm) ball. Roll it between your hands to shape it, pressing down a bit to remove any air pockets. Repeat until the mixture is used up.

4. In a 3-quart (2.8 L) pot over medium-high heat, heat about 2 inches (5 cm) of vegetable oil, keeping the temperature between 350°F and 375°F (180°C and 190°C).

5. Place the remaining ½ cup (62 g) of flour into a shallow bowl. In a second shallow bowl, stir together the ground flaxseed and hot water until blended. Place the panko in a third shallow bowl.

6. Roll each ball in the flour to coat evenly and then in the flaxseed mixture, turning to coat well. Drop the balls in the panko and roll around to coat evenly.

7. Line a wire rack with paper towels and set aside. Working in batches, place the balls into the hot oil and fry, rolling them around so they brown evenly, until golden brown and crisp. Transfer to the prepared rack to drain. Let cool for 1 minute before serving.

Makes 8 balls

CHEESY MAC MUFFINS

2 tablespoons (28 g) vegan butter, plus more for preparing the muffin tin
2 tablespoons (14 g) dried bread crumbs
2 cups (210 g) elbow macaroni
3 scallions, white and green parts, minced
3 tablespoons (23 g) all-purpose flour
½ teaspoon salt
¼ teaspoon ground black pepper
⅓ cup (20 g) nutritional yeast
1 teaspoon Dijon mustard
2 cups (480 ml) plain unsweetened nondairy milk
2 teaspoons fresh lemon juice

Try these muffins at your next brunch or make them to bring along to work or school for a yummy lunch. The addition of chopped cooked broccoli or other veggies makes them even better.

1. Preheat the oven to 375°F (190°C). Coat a nonstick muffin pan with butter.

2. Divide the bread crumbs evenly among the bottoms of the cups. Shake and tilt the pan to coat the cups on the bottoms and sides. Discard any excess crumbs.

3. Bring a large pot of salted water to a boil over high heat. Add the pasta and cook according to the package directions until al dente. Drain well and return to the pot. Set aside.

4. In a saucepan over medium heat, melt the butter.

5. Add the scallions and cook for 1 minute. Whisk in the flour, salt, and pepper and cook, whisking, for 1 minute.

6. Add the nutritional yeast and mustard and then whisk in the milk. Bring to a boil. Reduce the heat to maintain a simmer and cook, whisking constantly, for 2 minutes, or until smooth and thickened. Stir in the lemon juice. Taste and adjust the seasoning, as needed. Pour the cheese sauce over the pasta and stir to coat. Divide the pasta mixture evenly among the muffin cups and press it down into the cups. Bake for 15 to 20 minutes.

7. Remove the muffin pan and set aside for 10 minutes. Run a knife around the outer edge of each muffin and then pop them out of the cups.

Makes 8 to 12 muffins

MAC UNCHEESE SANDWICH

½ cup (weight varies) leftover or
    homemade mac uncheese, warmed
Vegan butter, for spreading
2 slices of bread
2 slices of vegan cheddar cheese
Sriracha or other hot sauce (optional)
3 thin tomato slices (optional)
½ cup (27 g) arugula, baby spinach, or
    other greens (optional)
3 slices cooked Tempeh Bacon (page
    87) or store-bought (optional)

If you're craving an easy lunch that is crunchy on the outside and gooey in the center, try this sandwich. Enjoy it as is or with the optional "BLT" additions. Instead of the oven, you can make your sandwich on a griddle or panini press.

1. Line a plate with parchment paper.

2. Spread the leftover mac uncheese into a 4 inch (10 cm) square on the prepared plate. Refrigerate to cool.

3. Preheat the oven to 500°F (250°C) and place a cast-iron, or other ovenproof, skillet inside to heat.

4. Spread the butter on one side of each slice of bread. Place the bread, buttered-side down, on a work surface and top one slice with one piece of cheese, sriracha (if using), the tomato slices (if using), the mac uncheese square, the arugula (if using), the tempeh bacon (if using), and the remaining slice of cheese. Cover the sandwich with the second slice of bread, butter-side out.

5. Wearing oven mitts, remove the skillet from the oven and place the sandwich in it. Bake until the cheese is melted, the bread is toasted, and the mac uncheese is hot, about 2 minutes. Cut the sandwich in half and serve hot.

Makes 1 sandwich

TIP

If you like the idea of mac uncheese in a sandwich, try it as a topping for veggie burgers, vegan hot dogs, and sloppy Joes. It also makes a good burrito filling when teamed with salsa and chili.

MAC 'N' PIZZA

Extra-virgin olive oil, for brushing

2½ to 3 cups (weight varies) leftover or homemade mac uncheese

1½ cups (345 g) Cheddary Sauce (page 103), divided

½ cup (120 ml) plain unsweetened nondairy milk

16 ounces (454 g) pizza dough, at room temperature

¼ teaspoon garlic powder

¼ teaspoon Italian seasoning

Salt, to taste

Ground black pepper, to taste

⅓ cup (75 g) chopped Tempeh Bacon (page 87) or other favorite pizza toppings (optional)

Chopped fresh parsley, for serving

People put everything on pizza these days, so why not mac uncheese? The optional sprinkling of chopped Tempeh Bacon really puts it over the top as an ultimate comfort food. If you don't have leftover mac uncheese, use the quick and easy recipe for One-Pot Cheesy Mac (page 39).

1. Preheat the oven to 425°F (220°C). Lightly brush a 12-inch (30 cm) round pizza pan with olive oil. Set aside.

2. In a saucepan over low heat, combine the mac uncheese and ½ cup (115 g) of the Cheddary Sauce, stirring to combine. Cook until heated through. If the mac uncheese is very firm, add up to ½ cup (120 ml) of milk to make it saucier and more spreadable. Keep warm.

3. Stretch the pizza dough into a 12-inch (30 cm) round and transfer to the prepared pizza pan. Brush the top of the dough with a little olive oil and sprinkle it with the garlic powder, Italian seasoning, salt, and pepper. Bake the crust until it begins to turn golden, about 10 minutes. Remove from the oven.

4. Spread ½ cup (115 g) of the Cheddary Sauce over the baked crust. Spread the macaroni and cheese on top of the sauce in an even layer, leaving a ½-inch (1 cm) border at the edge. Top with the Tempeh Bacon (if using) and the remaining ½ cup (115 g) of Cheddary Sauce. Bake until the crust is golden, about 10 minutes. Sprinkle with parsley and serve hot.

Makes 4 to 6 servings

MAC UNCHEESE QUESADILLAS

4 (10-inch, or 25 cm) flour tortillas
2½ to 3 cups (weight varies) leftover or
　　homemade mac uncheese, warmed
1 to 1½ cups (260 to 390 g) hot or mild
　　tomato salsa

This is a delicious way to stretch a small amount of leftover mac uncheese into a hearty meal for four. Instead of salsa, you could add cooked chopped spinach or broccoli. Or to pack an extra flavor punch, use the Salsa Mac and Queso (page 57) to make these quesadillas.

1. Arrange the tortillas on a work surface. Evenly distribute the macaroni uncheese over half of each tortilla. Top with equal amounts of salsa.

2. Heat a large nonstick skillet or griddle over medium heat. Arrange one tortilla, toppings up, in the skillet and cook for 1 minute, or until the tortilla begins to turn golden on the bottom. Using a spatula, fold the tortilla in half and cook for 1 minute more, or until golden brown. Flip and cook for 30 seconds more, or until golden brown. Repeat with the remaining tortillas. Slice each tortilla in half and serve immediately.

Makes 4 servings

INDIAN VERMICELLI PUDDING

1 tablespoon (14 g) vegan butter

1½ cups (168 g) broken (2- to 3-inch, or 5 to 7.5 cm) pieces vermicelli

3 cups (720 ml) plain unsweetened nondairy milk

¼ cup (50 g) sugar, plus more as needed

½ teaspoon ground cardamom

¼ cup (32 g) plus 2 tablespoons (16 g) crushed pistachios, or ¼ cup (35 g) plus 2 tablespoons (16 g) roasted cashews, divided

2 to 3 tablespoons (18 to 27 g) golden raisins

Serve hot, warm, or cold. The recipe can be easily doubled or tripled. The amount of vermicelli can be decreased or increased. If you add more, the consistency will be much thicker, more like a thick pudding.

1. In a saucepan over medium heat, melt the butter.

2. Add the vermicelli and cook, stirring, until golden brown, about 3 minutes.

3. Pour in the milk and bring just to a boil.

4. Stir in the sugar, cardamom, ¼ cup (32 g) of the pistachios, and the raisins. Reduce the heat to maintain a low simmer and cook, stirring occasionally, for about 5 minutes, or until the vermicelli is cooked and the milk is slightly thickened. Taste and add a little more sugar, as needed. Continue to cook for 2 to 3 minutes more, or until the desired consistency is reached. Transfer to a 3½-quart (3.3 L) serving dish. Sprinkle with the remaining 2 tablespoons (16 g) of pistachios.

Makes 4 to 6 servings

SWEET NOODLE KUGEL

4 tablespoons (56 g) vegan butter, plus
more for preparing the baking dish

16 ounces (454 g) fettuccine, or egg-
free noodles, broken in half

1 cup (140 g) unsalted raw cashews,
soaked in boiling water for
30 minutes and drained

8 ounces (225 g) soft tofu, drained, or
1 cup (240 g) vegan sour cream

⅓ cup (67 g) sugar

¼ cup (60 ml) plain unsweetened
nondairy milk

¼ cup (80 g) pure maple syrup

1 tablespoon (15 ml) fresh lemon juice

2 teaspoons vanilla extract

1 teaspoon ground cinnamon

1 cup (195 g) crushed pineapple,
drained

½ cup (60 g) dried cranberries

½ cup (55 g) chopped pecans, divided

This dairy-free sweet noodle kugel is made with a creamy cashew and tofu base and studded with pineapple, dried cranberries, and pecans. Use fettucine noodles, broken in half, or egg-free egg noodles, if you can find them.

1. Preheat the oven to 350°F (180°C). Coat a 4-quart (3.8 L) baking dish with butter. Set aside.

2. Bring a large pot of salted water to a boil over high heat. Add the pasta and cook according to the package directions until al dente. Drain well and return to the pot.

3. In a high-speed blender, combine the butter, cashews, tofu, sugar, milk, maple syrup, lemon juice, vanilla, and cinnamon. Blend until smooth. Add the sauce to the cooked noodles, along with the pineapple, cranberries, and ¼ cup (27 g) of the pecans. Stir to combine. Transfer the mixture to the prepared baking dish, smoothing the top. Sprinkle with the remaining pecans. Loosely cover the baking dish with aluminum foil and bake for 40 minutes.

4. Remove the foil and bake for 10 minutes more, or until golden.

5. Remove and let cool for at least 10 minutes. Cut into squares to serve.

Makes 4 to 6 servings

ACKNOWLEDGMENTS

I begin by acknowledging the vegan community as a whole for raising vegan mac and cheese to a cult-like status. It is their unbridled enthusiasm for this comfort food dish that inspired me to write *Vegan Mac & Cheese*.

A tremendous amount of gratitude goes to a recipe tester most cookbook authors can only dream about: Eve-Marie Williams, who single-handedly tested all of the recipes for this cookbook—that's a LOT of mac uncheese! I can't thank her enough for her dedication and commitment to helping me perfect these recipes.

I also wish to thank the terrific team at The Quarto Group/The Harvard Common Press, including Meredith Quinn and Anne Re for their part in making this book a reality, and especially Dan Rosenberg for championing the project from the beginning.

My enduring gratitude goes to my amazing literary agent for the past twenty years, Stacey Glick of Dystel, Goderich, and Bourret.

Thanks also to my dear friends Elissa Free and Bill Nooter, for being enthusiastic cheerleaders (and taste-testers!) for this project.

And, finally, immeasurable love and appreciation go to my husband, Jon, and my fabulous felines, for always being there for me.

ABOUT THE AUTHOR

Robin Robertson has worked with food for over thirty years as a restaurant chef, cooking teacher, and food writer. A longtime vegan, Robin is the author of more than twenty-five cookbooks, including the best-selling *Vegan Planet*, *Fresh from the Vegan Slow Cooker*, *One-Dish Vegan*, *1,000 Vegan Recipes*, and *Quick-Fix Vegan*.

Robin wrote the Global Vegan column for *VegNews* magazine for ten years and has also written for *Vegetarian Times* and *Cooking Light*, among others.

In addition to writing her own cookbooks, she has also written recipes for several well-known authors, including *The How Not to Die Cookbook* by Michael Greger, M.D., with Gene Stone.

Robin is active on all major social media outlets. Her website is robinrobertson.com.

INDEX

Note: Page references in *italics* indicate photographs.

ALSO AVAILABLE

One-Dish Vegan Revised and Expanded Edition
978-1-55832-942-3

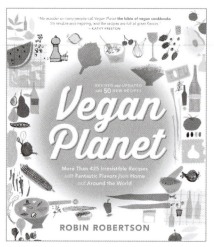

Vegan Planet, Revised Edition
978-1-55832-831-0

Fresh from the Vegan Slow Cooker
978-1-55832-790-0